ENDORSEMENTS

There is nothing more important in the Christian life than spending quality time with the Lord daily, and then living out what He teaches us every day of our lives. In the midst of the busy world, we live in, such a practice is often ignored, neglect, or rushed. I am thankful for Joe Pace's efforts in this book to help us develop a habit of absorbing God's Word through mediating on concentrated devotion. May all of us grow through the practices shown forth in this work. We cannot help but be encouraged by it!

Dr. Daniel R. Heeringa
Senior Pastor First Baptist Church Pickens, SC

This book is very practical and will be a great tool and help to every Christian.

Rev. Scott Willis
Pastor, Mountain View Baptist Church

Pascal said, "There is a God-shaped vacuum in the heart of each man which cannot be satisfied by any created thing but only by God the Creator, made known through Jesus Christ."

In his book, the author helps the reader focus on issues of the heart through scripture and personal reflection. If you desire to grow closer to God and to know His purpose for your life, you must be willing to let God speak into your life through His Word. The Biblical truths shared and the spiritually probing questions asked in this book will lead you to a closer walk with God and a better understanding of your purpose according to God's perfect will for your life.

James 4:8(NLT) is a promise to you. It says, "Come close to God, and God will come close to you".

May this book bring you closer to God.

Rev. Rick Hayes
Associational Missions Strategist
Pickens Twelve Mile Baptist Association

One of the missing ingredients in most Christians life today is that we don't spend adequate time in a quiet place and time to hear from GOD. I believe Joe Pace is right on target calling all Christians and the church to make it a priority to get alone with GOD and mediate on HIS Word as we claim HIS promises and keep HIS commandments.

I know that if we will take to heart and apply these truths to our lives it will make a difference in us personally and as a church and the kingdom of GOD.

Dr. David Gallamore
PASTOR ROCK SPRINGS BAPTIST CHURCH
EASLEY S. C.

"Rev. Joe Pace" because he is a preacher, "Preacher Joe" because he is my church's pastor, and just "Joe" because he is a friend. Whatever name you know him by, his over 50 years in ministry has allowed him to learn a thing or two about getting closer to God. Time spent in quiet meditation and prayer is something woefully lacking in the life of most Christians. The principles taught here will help the reader develop a deeper and more meaningful relationship with God. And that's one of the main desires of a Christian, isn't it? It sure should be.

Tomas B. Hannah
Minister of Music Shady Grove Baptist Church

GETTING CLOSER TO GOD USING MEDITATION

Joseph Pace

WestBow Press books may be ordered through booksellers or by contacting:

WestBow Press
A Division of Thomas Nelson & Zondervan
1663 Liberty Drive
Bloomington, IN 47403
www.westbowpress.com
844-714-3454

Interior Image Credit: Joe Pace & Diana Grove

ISBN: 978-1-9736-9966-8 (sc)
ISBN: 978-1-9736-9967-5 (e)

Library of Congress Control Number: 2023909870

Print information available on the last page.

WestBow Press rev. date: 06/09/2023

GETTING HELPFUL HINTS TO AID US TO GET CLOSER TO GOD USING MEDITATION

I need to get closer to God.

Perhaps you need to also.

LET'S LOOK AT ONE WAY THAT COULD GREATLY HELP.

JOSEPH PACE

Dedication

THIS BOOK IS DEDICATED TO MY WIFE
LOUISE AND DAUGHTER MICHELE.

AND TO OTHERS WHO HELPED ME GROW IN FAITH.

ACKNOWLEDGEMENTS

I wish to thank Stephen Rice, Georgette Gallo, Leandra Drummy and all the staff at WESTBOW, and those who endorsed my book.

Introduction

There are few who would dare say they are close to the Lord. Sad but true. Do we desire to get closer to Him? This book with God's blessing can help us get closer to Him.

Let's get started now.

FIRST, get in a private place, such as a room or somewhere outside where it is quiet as possible.

Use your phone to play soft easy instrumental music OR play soft falling water or the sounds of a creek, OR maybe no sound may help.

Get comfortable.

Be Still

Relax- YOU MAY RELAX-

Slowly START AT THE TOP OF YOUR HEAD

Then your HANDS,

Next your ARMS,

Then your MID SECTION,

Relax your LEGS completely,

AND now your FEET.

Relax

Now Focus

Free your mind of all thoughts

Listen or read a thought from the Meditations on Matthew.

THINK ON A THOUGHT FROM MEDIATIONS ON MATTHEW

Dwell on one thought at a time, and take as much time as you need before going on to the next meditation.

No hurry just deeply dwell on that meditation.

Think, pray, dwell on just that thought.

SAY EACH MEDITATION THREE TIMES AND CONTINUE SLOWLY.

You may desire to write down notes as you mediate or after you do so.

You may desire to read the whole chapter before you meditate.

Underline words that jump out at you may help.

MAYBE EVEN CLOSE YOUR EYES.

I am using the Holman Christian Standard Version for the first 10 chapters to help everyone better understand in simple English.

ASK YOURSELF, "GOD WHAT ARE YOU SAYING TO ME AS I MEDIATE?

MATTHEW 1

The Genealogy of Jesus Christ

*1 The historical record of Jesus Christ, the
Son of David, the Son of Abraham:*

From Abraham to David

2 Abraham fathered Isaac,

Isaac fathered Jacob,

Jacob fathered Judah and his brothers,

I have left out verses 3-14, you may desire to read those for yourself, they are part of the family tree of Jesus' earthly father Joseph.

*15 Eliud fathered Eleazar,
Eleazar fathered Matthan,
Matthan fathered Jacob,*

*16 and Jacob fathered Joseph the husband of Mary,
who gave birth to Jesus who is called the Messiah.*

*17 So all the generations from Abraham to David were 14 generations;
and from David until the exile to Babylon, 14 generations; and
from the exile to Babylon until the Messiah, 14 generations.*

The Nativity of the Messiah

*18 The birth of Jesus Christ came about this way: After His mother
Mary had been engaged to Joseph, it was discovered before they
came together that she was pregnant by the Holy Spirit. 19 So*

her husband Joseph, being a righteous man, and not wanting to disgrace her publicly, decided to divorce her secretly.

20 But after he had considered these things, an angel of the
Lord suddenly appeared to him in a dream, saying, "Joseph,
son of David, don't be afraid to take Mary as your wife,
because what has been conceived in her is by the Holy Spirit.
21 She will give birth to a son, and you are to name Him
Jesus, because He will save His people from their sins."

22 Now all this took place to fulfill what was
spoken by the Lord through the prophet:

23 See, the virgin will become pregnant
and give birth to a son,
and they will name Him Immanuel,
which is translated "God is with us."

24 When Joseph got up from sleeping, he did as the Lord's angel
had commanded him. He married her. 25 but did not know her
intimately until she gave birth to a son. And he named Him Jesus.

<u>Now let's mediate.</u>

<u>Family is important.</u>

ALLOW ME TO SHARE MY THOUGHTS ON THIS ONE.

Allow me to give you my meditation on that thought.

The gospel of Matthew takes up so much space giving the family history of Jesus-why? No doubt to show us the importance of the family.

How are my family relationships?

What is my role in my family?

What can I do to make things in my family better?

Does my family know how I look to them for support and help?

Am I doing what I can to make my family what it needs to be?

God help us.

Now your time, mediate on

Family is important.

Childbirth is very important.

FAMILY IS GOD'S PLAN

MY FAMILY IS IMPORTANT

MY FAMILY CAN BE A BLESSING

I CAN HELP MY FAMILY BE A BLESSING

GOD HELP MY FAMILY

CHILDBIRTH IS ALSO IMPORTANT.

The ideal family is husband and wife.

Names matter.

Bibles can be helpful.

What can I do to make my meditation better?

What was my highlight from meditating on this chapter.

1

WISE MEN SEEK THE KING

1 After Jesus was born in Bethlehem of Judea in the days of King
Herod, wise men from the east arrived unexpectedly in Jerusalem,
2 saying, "Where is He who has been born King of the Jews? For
we saw His star in the east and have come to worship Him."

3 When King Herod heard this, he was deeply disturbed, and all
Jerusalem with him. 4 So he assembled all the chief priests and scribes
of the people and asked them where the Messiah would be born.

5 "In Bethlehem of Judea," they told him, "because
this is what was written by the prophet:

6 And you, Bethlehem, in the land of Judah,

are by no means least among the leaders of Judah:

because out of you will come a leader

who will shepherd My people Israel."

7 Then Herod secretly summoned the wise men and asked them
the exact time the star appeared. 8 He sent them to Bethlehem
and said, "Go and search carefully for the child. When you find
Him, report back to me so that I too can go and worship Him."

*9 After hearing the king, they went on their way. And there it was —
the star they had seen in the east! It led them until it came and stopped
above the place where the child was. 10 When they saw the star, they
were overjoyed beyond measure. 11 Entering the house, they saw the
child with Mary His mother, and falling to their knees, they worshiped
Him. Then they opened their treasures and presented Him with gifts:
gold, frankincense, and myrrh. 12 And being warned in a dream not to
go back to Herod, they returned to their own country by another route.*

The Flight into Egypt

*13 After they were gone, an angel of the Lord suddenly appeared to
Joseph in a dream, saying, "Get up! Take the child and His mother,
flee to Egypt, and stay there until I tell you. For Herod is about to
search for the child to destroy Him." 14 So he got up, took the child
and His mother during the night, and escaped to Egypt. 15 He stayed
there until Herod's death, so that what was spoken by the Lord
through the prophet might be fulfilled: Out of Egypt I called My Son.*

The Massacre of the Innocents

*16 Then Herod, when he saw that he had been outwitted
by the wise men, flew into a rage. He gave orders to
massacre all the male children in and around Bethlehem
who were two years old and under, in keeping with the
time he had learned from the wise men. 17 Then what was
spoken through Jeremiah the prophet was fulfilled:*

*18 A voice was heard in Ramah,
weeping, and great mourning,
Rachel weeping for her children;
and she refused to be consoled,
because they were no more.*

The Holy Family in Nazareth

19 After Herod died, an angel of the Lord suddenly appeared in
a dream to Joseph in Egypt, 20 saying, "Get up! Take the child
and His mother and go to the land of Israel, because those who
sought the child's life are dead." 21 So he got up, took the child
and His mother, and entered the land of Israel. 22 But when
he heard that Archelaus was ruling over Judea in place of his
father Herod, he was afraid to go there. And being warned in a
dream, he withdrew to the region of Galilee. 23 Then he went
and settled in a town called Nazareth to fulfill what was spoken
through the prophets, that He will be called a Nazarene.

<u>Now, time to mediate.</u>

Wise people still look for Jesus until they find Him.

The government doesn't know all it needs to.

It helps to ask questions.

Sometimes lies are told.

I need to rejoice more

WHAT AM I looking for

What is important to me?

How does God speak?

How does God speak to me?

DO I know when to flee?

What should I flee from?

Wrong doesn't make right.

Where could God lead me?

What was my highlight from meditating on this chapter?

2

The Messiah's Herald

1 In those days John the Baptist came, preaching in the
Wilderness of Judea 2 and saying, "Repent, because the
kingdom of heaven has come near!" 3 For he is the one
spoken of through the prophet Isaiah, who said:

A voice of one crying out in the wilderness:

Prepare the way for the Lord;
make His paths straight!

4 John himself had a camel-hair garment with a leather belt
around his waist, and his food was locusts and wild honey.
5 Then people from Jerusalem, all Judea, and all the vicinity
of the Jordan were flocking to him, 6 and they were baptized
by him in the Jordan River as they confessed their sins.

7 When he saw many of the Pharisees and Sadducees coming to
the place of his baptism, he said to them, "Brood of vipers! Who
warned you to flee from the coming wrath? 8 Therefore produce fruit
consistent with repentance. 9 And don't presume to say to yourselves,
'We have Abraham as our father.' For I tell you that God is able to
raise up children for Abraham from these stones! 10 Even now the
ax is ready to strike the root of the trees! Therefore, every tree that
doesn't produce good fruit will be cut down and thrown into the fire.

11 "I baptize you with water for repentance, but the One who
is coming after me is more powerful than I. I am not worthy to
remove His sandals. He Himself will baptize you with the Holy
Spirit and fire. 12 His winnowing shovel is in His hand, and He
will clear His threshing floor and gather His wheat into the barn.
But the chaff He will burn up with fire that never goes out."

The Baptism of Jesus

13 Then Jesus came from Galilee to John at the Jordan, to be
baptized by him. 14 But John tried to stop Him, saying, "I
need to be baptized by You, and yet You come to me?"

15 Jesus answered him, "Allow it for now, because this is the way for
us to fulfill all righteousness." Then he allowed Him to be baptized.

16 After Jesus was baptized, He went up immediately from
the water. The heavens suddenly opened for Him, and He
saw the Spirit of God descending like a dove and coming
down on Him. 17 And there came a voice from heaven:

This is My beloved Son.

I take delight in Him!

Now mediate.

What does God want me to do?

How can I serve God now?

What do I need to repent of?

Will I allow God to have his way with me?

Do I listen to good preaching and teaching?

Is Jesus coming soon?

What do I love to eat?

Have I been baptized?

Have I confessed my sins?

Do I enjoy being with godly people?

Not everyone goes to church for the right reason.

Am I humble?

How can I be better?

How important is Jesus to me?

Do I please God? When? How? How often?

What was the main thing that spoke to me as I read this chapter?

3

THE TEMPTATION OF JESUS

1 Then Jesus was led up by the Spirit into the wilderness to be
tempted by the Devil. 2 After He had fasted 40 days and 40 nights,
He was hungry. 3 Then the tempter approached Him and said,
"If You are the Son of God, tell these stones to become bread."

4 But He answered, "It is written:
Man must not live on bread alone
but on every word that comes
from the mouth of God."

5 Then the Devil took Him to the holy city, had Him stand
on the pinnacle of the temple, 6 and said to Him, "If You are
the Son of God, throw Yourself down. For it is written:

He will give His angels orders concerning you,
and they will support you with their hands
so that you will not strike
your foot against a stone."

7 Jesus told him, "It is also written: Do not test the Lord your God."

8 Again, the Devil took Him to a very high mountain and showed Him
all the kingdoms of the world and their splendor. 9 And he said to Him,
"I will give You all these things if You will fall down and worship me."

*10 Then Jesus told him, "Go away, Satan! For it is written:
Worship the Lord your God,
and serve only Him."*

*11 Then the Devil left Him, and immediately
angels came and began to serve Him.*

Ministry in Galilee

*12 When He heard that John had been arrested, He withdrew
into Galilee. 13 He left Nazareth behind and went to live in
Capernaum by the sea, in the region of Zebulun and Naphtali. 14
This was to fulfill what was spoken through the prophet Isaiah:*

*15 Land of Zebulun and land of Naphtali,
along the sea road, beyond the Jordan,
Galilee of the Gentiles!*

*16 The people who live in darkness
have seen a great light,
and for those living in the shadowland of death,
light has dawned.*

*17 From then on Jesus began to preach, "Repent,
because the kingdom of heaven has come near!"*

The First Disciples

*18 As He was walking along the Sea of Galilee, He saw two
brothers, Simon, who was called Peter, and his brother Andrew.
They were casting a net into the sea, since they were fishermen.
19 "Follow Me," He told them, "and I will make you fish for
people!" 20 Immediately they left their nets and followed Him.*

21 Going on from there, He saw two other brothers, James the son of Zebedee, and his brother John. They were in a boat with Zebedee their father, mending their nets, and He called them. 22 Immediately they left the boat and their father and followed Him.

Teaching, Preaching, and Healing

23 Jesus was going all over Galilee, teaching in their synagogues, preaching the good news of the kingdom, and healing every disease and sickness among the people. 24 Then the news about Him spread throughout Syria. So they brought to Him all those who were afflicted, those suffering from various diseases and intense pains, the demon-possessed, the epileptics, and the paralytics. And He healed them. 25 Large crowds followed Him from Galilee, Decapolis, Jerusalem, Judea, and beyond the Jordan.

Now mediate.

Where might the Holy Spirit lead me?

Have I ever fasted?

How important is the Bible to me?

How important should the Bible be to me?

Life has problems.

The devil bothers everyone.

Do I temp God?

I need to be careful how I understand and apply the bible to my life?

I have been mistreated.

Everyone has been mistreated.

The Old Testament is very important.

What do I see?

Do I see people or a crowd?

What do I look for?

What have I learned as I get older?

Jesus walked much- I should too.

Jesus challenged people.

Am I following Jesus?

Do I study Jesus' teachings?

When have I helped someone?

People enjoyed being with Jesus.

What was my highlight from meditating on this chapter?

4

THE SERMON ON THE MOUNT

1 When He saw the crowds, He went up on the
mountain, and after He sat down, *His disciples came*
to Him. 2 *Then He began to teach them, saying:*

The Beatitudes

3 *"The poor in spirit are blessed,*
for the kingdom of heaven is theirs.

4 *Those who mourn are blessed,*
for they will be comforted.

5 *The gentle are blessed,*
for they will inherit the earth.

6 *Those who hunger and thirst for righteousness are blessed,*
for they will be filled.

7 *The merciful are blessed,*
for they will be shown mercy.

8 *The pure in heart are blessed,*
for they will see God.

9 *The peacemakers are blessed,*
for they will be called sons of God.

*10 Those who are persecuted for righteousness are blessed,
for the kingdom of heaven is theirs.*

*11 "You are blessed when they insult and persecute you and
falsely say every kind of evil against you because of Me. 12 Be
glad and rejoice, because your reward is great in heaven. For
that is how they persecuted the prophets who were before you.*

Believers Are Salt and Light

*13 "You are the salt of the earth. But if the salt should lose
its taste, how can it be made salty? It's no longer good for
anything but to be thrown out and trampled on by men.*

*14 "You are the light of the world. A city situated on a
hill cannot be hidden. 15 No one lights a lamp and puts
it under a basket, but rather on a lampstand, and it gives
light for all who are in the house. 16 In the same way, let
your light shine before men, so that they may see your
good works and give glory to your Father in heaven.*

Christ Fulfills the Law

*17 "Don't assume that I came to destroy the Law or the Prophets.
I did not come to destroy but to fulfill. 18 For I assure you:
Until heaven and earth pass away, not the smallest letter or
one stroke of a letter will pass from the law until all things are
accomplished. 19 Therefore, whoever breaks one of the least of
these commands and teaches people to do so will be called least in
the kingdom of heaven. But whoever practices and teaches these
commands will be called great in the kingdom of heaven. 20 For
I tell you, unless your righteousness surpasses that of the scribes
and Pharisees, you will never enter the kingdom of heaven.*

Murder Begins in the Heart

21 "You have heard that it was said to our ancestors, Do not
murder, and whoever murders will be subject to judgment. 22 But
I tell you, everyone who is angry with his brother will be subject to
judgment. And whoever says to his brother, 'Fool!' will be subject
to the Sanhedrin. But whoever says, 'You moron!' will be subject
to hellfire. 23 So if you are offering your gift on the altar, and there
you remember that your brother has something against you, 24
leave your gift there in front of the altar. First go and be reconciled
with your brother, and then come and offer your gift. 25 Reach a
settlement quickly with your adversary while you're on the way with
him, or your adversary will hand you over to the judge, the judge
to the officer, and you will be thrown into prison. 26 I assure you:
You will never get out of there until you have paid the last penny!

Adultery in the Heart

27 "You have heard that it was said, Do not commit adultery. 28
But I tell you, everyone who looks at a woman to lust for her has
already committed adultery with her in his heart. 29 If your right
eye causes you to sin, gouge it out and throw it away. For it is better
that you lose one of the parts of your body than for your whole
body to be thrown into hell. 30 And if your right hand causes you
to sin, cut it off and throw it away. For it is better that you lose one
of the parts of your body than for your whole body to go into hell!

Divorce Practices Censured

31 "It was also said, Whoever divorces his wife must give her a
written notice of divorce. 32 But I tell you, everyone who divorces
his wife, except in a case of sexual immorality, causes her to commit
adultery. And whoever marries a divorced woman commits adultery.

Tell the Truth

33 "Again, you have heard that it was said to our ancestors, You
must not break your oath, but you must keep your oaths to the
Lord. 34 But I tell you, don't take an oath at all: either by heaven,
because it is God's throne; 35 or by the earth, because it is His
footstool; or by Jerusalem, because it is the city of the great King. 36
Neither should you swear by your head, because you cannot make
a single hair white or black. 37 But let your word 'yes' be 'yes,' and
your 'no' be 'no.' Anything more than this is from the evil one.

Go the Second Mile

38 "You have heard that it was said, An eye for an eye and a tooth
for a tooth. 39 But I tell you, don't resist an evildoer. On the contrary,
if anyone slaps you on your right cheek, turn the other to him also.
40 As for the one who wants to sue you and take away your shirt,
let him have your coat as well. 41 And if anyone forces you to go
one mile, go with him two. 42 Give to the one who asks you, and
don't turn away from the one who wants to borrow from you.

Love Your Enemies

43 "You have heard that it was said, Love your neighbor and hate
your enemy. 44 But I tell you, love your enemies and pray for those
who persecute you, 45 so that you may be sons of your Father in
heaven. For He causes His sun to rise on the evil and the good, and
sends rain on the righteous and the unrighteous. 46 For if you love
those who love you, what reward will you have? Don't even the tax
collectors do the same? 47 And if you greet only your brothers, what
are you doing out of the ordinary? Don't even the Gentiles do the
same? 48 Be perfect, therefore, as your heavenly Father is perfect.

Mediate.

I need to know what Jesus taught.

How can I learn what Jesus taught?

Blessings come to those who heed what Jesus said.

I can be happy.

Do I know how to rejoice?

People loved Jesus.

The Bible is helpful and true.

Anger hurts everyone badly.

Is there good anger?

What do I spend my money on?

I must be careful how I treat others.

Am I a disciplined person?

Can I say no?

Can God use me?

Marriage is a serious thing.

Does my word have great value?

Do I mean what I say?

Do I do more than expected?

What do I love the most?

Who do I love the most?

Do I love other people?

Do I only love myself?

How close to perfect am I?

From this chapter which meditation spoke the most to me?

5

How to Give

1 "Be careful not to practice your righteousness in front of people,
to be seen by them. Otherwise, you will have no reward from your
Father in heaven. 2 So whenever you give to the poor, don't sound
a trumpet before you, as the hypocrites do in the synagogues and
on the streets, to be applauded by people. I assure you: They've got
their reward! 3 But when you give to the poor, don't let your left
hand know what your right hand is doing, 4 so that your giving may
be in secret. And your Father who sees in secret will reward you.

How to Pray

5 "Whenever you pray, you must not be like the hypocrites, because
they love to pray standing in the synagogues and on the street corners
to be seen by people. I assure you: They've got their reward! 6 But when
you pray, go into your private room, shut your door, and pray to your
Father who is in secret. And your Father who sees in secret will reward
you. 7 When you pray, don't babble like the idolaters, since they
imagine they'll be heard for their many words. 8 Don't be like them,
because your Father knows the things you need before you ask Him.

The Model Prayer

9 "Therefore, you should pray like this:
Our Father in heaven,
Your name be honored as holy.

10 Your kingdom come.
Your will be done
on earth as it is in heaven.

11 Give us today our daily bread.

12 And forgive us our debts,
as we also have forgiven our debtors.

13 And do not bring us into temptation,
but deliver us from the evil one.
[For Yours is the kingdom and the power
and the glory forever. Amen.]

14 "For if you forgive people their wrongdoing, your heavenly
Father will forgive you as well. 15 But if you don't forgive
people, your Father will not forgive your wrongdoing.

How to Fast

16 "Whenever you fast, don't be sad-faced like the hypocrites.
For they make their faces unattractive so their fasting is obvious
to people. I assure you: They've got their reward! 17 But when
you fast, put oil on your head, and wash your face, 18 so that
you don't show your fasting to people but to your Father who is
in secret. And your Father who sees in secret will reward you.

God and Possessions

19 "Don't collect for yourselves treasures on earth, where moth
and rust destroy and where thieves break in and steal. 20 But
collect for yourselves treasures in heaven, where neither moth
nor rust destroys, and where thieves don't break in and steal.
21 For where your treasure is, there your heart will be also.

22 "The eye is the lamp of the body. If your eye is good,
your whole body will be full of light. 23 But if your eye is
bad, your whole body will be full of darkness. So if the light
within you is darkness — how deep is that darkness!

24 "No one can be a slave of two masters, since either he will
hate one and love the other, or be devoted to one and despise
the other. You cannot be slaves of God and of money.

The Cure for Anxiety

25 "This is why I tell you: Don't worry about your life, what you
will eat or what you will drink; or about your body, what you will
wear. Isn't life more than food and the body more than clothing?
26 Look at the birds of the sky: They don't sow or reap or gather
into barns, yet your heavenly Father feeds them. Aren't you
worth more than they? 27 Can any of you add a single cubit to
his height by worrying? 28 And why do you worry about clothes?
Learn how the wildflowers of the field grow: they don't labor or
spin thread. 29 Yet I tell you that not even Solomon in all his
splendor was adorned like one of these! 30 If that's how God
clothes the grass of the field, which is here today and thrown into
the furnace tomorrow, won't He do much more for you — you
of little faith? 31 So don't worry, saying, 'What will we eat?' or
'What will we drink?' or 'What will we wear?' 32 For the idolaters
eagerly seek all these things, and your heavenly Father knows
that you need them. 33 But seek first the kingdom of God and
His righteousness, and all these things will be provided for you.
34 Therefore don't worry about tomorrow, because tomorrow
will worry about itself. Each day has enough trouble of its own.

Mediation time.

What do I do to help others?

What will my reward in heaven look like?

What do I need to do to be a better person?

God loves me.

How do I show that I love God?

When do I pray?

Do I only pray in emergencies?

Do I have a place of prayer?

When is the last time I had a good talk with Jesus?

I need to pray, help me oh God.

God is everywhere.

Am I a cheerleader for God or Satan?

God can forgive me.

Do I give God honor and glory?

Who have I forgiven?

What do I do to be a blessing?

Is God pleased at what I look at?

Am I a full time Christian?

Do I worry?

What does God think about me?

How much faith do I have?

Am I seeking God?

Do I desire to live right?

Live right and be blessed.

Do I live one day at a time?

Do I live in the moment?

In this chapter what did I learn?

6

Do Not Judge

1 "Do not judge, so that you won't be judged. 2 For with the
judgment you use, you will be judged, and with the measure
you use, it will be measured to you. 3 Why do you look at the
speck in your brother's eye but don't notice the log in your
own eye? 4 Or how can you say to your brother, 'Let me take
the speck out of your eye,' and look, there's a log in your eye? 5
Hypocrite! First take the log out of your eye, and then you will
see clearly to take the speck out of your brother's eye. 6 Don't
give what is holy to dogs or toss your pearls before pigs, or they
will trample them with their feet, turn, and tear you to pieces.

Keep Asking, Searching, Knocking

7 "Keep asking, and it will be given to you. Keep searching,
and you will find. Keep knocking, and the door will be
opened to you. 8 For everyone who asks receives, and
the one who searches finds, and to the one who knocks,
the door will be opened. 9 What man among you, if
his son asks him for bread, will give him a stone? 10
Or if he asks for a fish, will give him a snake? 11 If you
then, who are evil, know how to give good gifts to your
children, how much more will your Father in heaven
give good things to those who ask Him! 12 Therefore,
whatever you want others to do for you, do also the
same for them — this is the Law and the Prophets.

Entering the Kingdom

13 "Enter through the narrow gate. For the gate is wide and
the road is broad that leads to destruction, and there are
many who go through it. 14 How narrow is the gate and
difficult the road that leads to life, and few find it.

15 "Beware of false prophets who come to you in sheep's clothing
but inwardly are ravaging wolves. 16 You'll recognize them by
their fruit. Are grapes gathered from thornbushes or figs from
thistles? 17 In the same way, every good tree produces good fruit,
but a bad tree produces bad fruit. 18 A good tree can't produce
bad fruit; neither can a bad tree produce good fruit. 19 Every
tree that doesn't produce good fruit is cut down and thrown
into the fire. 20 So you'll recognize them by their fruit.

21 "Not everyone who says to Me, 'Lord, Lord!' will enter the
kingdom of heaven, but only the one who does the will of My Father
in heaven. 22 On that day many will say to Me, 'Lord, Lord, didn't
we prophesy in Your name, drive out demons in Your name, and
do many miracles in Your name?' 23 Then I will announce to
them, 'I never knew you! Depart from Me, you lawbreakers!'

The Two Foundations

24 "Therefore, everyone who hears these words of Mine and acts on
them will be like a sensible man who built his house on the rock.
25 The rain fell, the rivers rose, and the winds blew and pounded
that house. Yet it didn't collapse, because its foundation was on
the rock. 26 But everyone who hears these words of Mine and
doesn't act on them will be like a foolish man who built his house
on the sand. 27 The rain fell, the rivers rose, the winds blew and
pounded that house, and it collapsed. And its collapse was great!"

28 When Jesus had finished this sermon, the crowds were astonished at His teaching, 29 because He was teaching them like one who had authority, and not like their scribes.

Time to mediate.

I Should not judge others, but I do-shame on me.

Others tend to treat me like I treat them.

It is easy to see the faults of others, but not mine.

We can't help some people, but I will try.

What we really desire, we often obtain.

Do I like to give?

There are better ways to live.

Not everything is good.

Watching what people do reveals much about them.

Does what I do matter?

Not everyone is going to heaven.

Is Jesus my savior?

Am I wise or foolish?

Troubles come to everyone. How do I handle them, or do they handle me?

What am I building IN MY LIFE?

Do I listen to what Jesus says?

Jesus knows what he is talking about.

What did I learn as I studied this chapter?

7

A Man Cleansed

1 When He came down from the mountain, large crowds
followed Him. 2 Right away a man with a serious skin
disease came up and knelt before Him, saying, "Lord,
if You are willing, You can make me clean."

3 Reaching out His hand He touched him, saying, "I am willing; be
made clean." Immediately his disease was healed. 4 Then Jesus told
him, "See that you don't tell anyone; but go, show yourself to the priest,
and offer the gift that Moses prescribed, as a testimony to them."

A Centurion's Faith

5 When He entered Capernaum, a centurion came
to Him, pleading with Him, 6 "Lord, my servant is
lying at home paralyzed, in terrible agony!"

7 "I will come and heal him," He told him.

8 "Lord," the centurion replied, "I am not worthy to have You
come under my roof. But only say the word, and my servant will be
cured. 9 For I too am a man under authority, having soldiers under
my command. I say to this one, 'Go!' and he goes; and to another,
'Come!' and he comes; and to my slave, 'Do this!' and he does it."

10 Hearing this, Jesus was amazed and said to those following
Him, "I assure you: I have not found anyone in Israel with so great

a faith! 11 I tell you that many will come from east and west, and
recline at the table with Abraham, Isaac, and Jacob in the kingdom
of heaven. 12 But the sons of the kingdom will be thrown into the
outer darkness. In that place there will be weeping and gnashing of
teeth." 13 Then Jesus told the centurion, "Go. As you have believed,
let it be done for you." And his servant was cured that very moment.

Healings at Capernaum

14 When Jesus went into Peter's house, He saw his mother-in-law
lying in bed with a fever. 15 So He touched her hand, and the fever
left her. Then she got up and began to serve Him. 16 When evening
came, they brought to Him many who were demon-possessed. He
drove out the spirits with a word and healed all who were sick, 17 so
that what was spoken through the prophet Isaiah might be fulfilled:

He Himself took our weaknesses
and carried our diseases.
Following Jesus

18 When Jesus saw large crowds around Him, He gave the order
to go to the other side of the sea. 19 A scribe approached Him
and said, "Teacher, I will follow You wherever You go!"

20 Jesus told him, "Foxes have dens and birds of the sky have
nests, but the Son of Man has no place to lay His head."

21 "Lord," another of His disciples said, "first let me go bury my father."

22 But Jesus told him, "Follow Me, and let
the dead bury their own dead."

Wind and Wave Obey the Master

23 As He got into the boat, His disciples followed Him. 24 Suddenly,
a violent storm arose on the sea, so that the boat was being swamped
by the waves. But He was sleeping. 25 So the disciples came and
woke Him up, saying, "Lord, save us! We're going to die!"

26 But He said to them, "Why are you fearful, you of
little faith?" Then He got up and rebuked the winds
and the sea. And there was a great calm.

27 The men were amazed and asked, "What kind of man
is this? — even the winds and the sea obey Him!"

Demons Driven Out by the Master

28 When He had come to the other side, to the region of the
Gadarenes, two demon-possessed men met Him as they came out
of the tombs. They were so violent that no one could pass that way.
29 Suddenly they shouted, "What do You have to do with us, Son
of God? Have You come here to torment us before the time?"

30 Now a long way off from them, a large herd of
pigs was feeding. 31 "If You drive us out," the demons
begged Him, "send us into the herd of pigs."

32 "Go!" He told them. So when they had come out, they entered
the pigs. And suddenly the whole herd rushed down the steep
bank into the sea and perished in the water. 33 Then the men who
tended them fled. They went into the city and reported everything
— especially what had happened to those who were demon-
possessed. 34 At that, the whole town went out to meet Jesus.
When they saw Him, they begged Him to leave their region.

Mediation time.

Am I good at socializing?

Do I follow Jesus or Satan?

Who or what do I worship?

How do I worship?

Jesus still heals-glory!

How do I help the kingdom of God?

Do others share their problems with me?

How do I handle concerns?

What kind of faith do I have?

Do I welcome others into my house?

Jesus still heals.

Am I following Jesus?

Jesus' powers are amazing.

The devil and his crowd are still very busy.

Some don't welcome Jesus.

8

The Son of Man Forgives and Heals

1 So He got into a boat, crossed over, and came to His own
town. 2 Just then some men brought to Him a paralytic
lying on a mat. Seeing their faith, Jesus told the paralytic,
"Have courage, son, your sins are forgiven."

3 At this, some of the scribes said among
themselves, "He's blaspheming!"

4 But perceiving their thoughts, Jesus said, "Why are you thinking
evil things in your hearts? 5 For which is easier: to say, 'Your sins are
forgiven,' or to say, 'Get up and walk'? 6 But so you may know that
the Son of Man has authority on earth to forgive sins" — then He told
the paralytic, "Get up, pick up your mat, and go home." 7 And he got
up and went home. 8 When the crowds saw this, they were awestruck
and gave glory to God who had given such authority to men.

The Call of Matthew

9 As Jesus went on from there, He saw a man named
Matthew sitting at the tax office, and He said to him,
"Follow Me!" So he got up and followed Him.

10 While He was reclining at the table in the house, many tax
collectors and sinners came as guests to eat with Jesus and His

disciples. 11 When the Pharisees saw this, they asked His disciples,
"Why does your Teacher eat with tax collectors and sinners?"

12 But when He heard this, He said, "Those who are well
don't need a doctor, but the sick do. 13 Go and learn
what this means: I desire mercy and not sacrifice. For
I didn't come to call the righteous, but sinners."

A Question about Fasting

14 Then John's disciples came to Him, saying, "Why do we and
the Pharisees fast often, but Your disciples do not fast?"

15 Jesus said to them, "Can the wedding guests be sad while the
groom is with them? The time will come when the groom will
be taken away from them, and then they will fast. 16 No one
patches an old garment with unshrunk cloth, because the patch
pulls away from the garment and makes the tear worse. 17 And
no one puts new wine into old wineskins. Otherwise, the skins
burst, the wine spills out, and the skins are ruined. But they
put new wine into fresh wineskins, and both are preserved."

A Girl Restored and a Woman Healed

18 As He was telling them these things, suddenly one of the
leaders came and knelt down before Him, saying, "My daughter
is near death, but come and lay Your hand on her, and she will
live." 19 So Jesus and His disciples got up and followed him.

20 Just then, a woman who had suffered from bleeding for 12 years
approached from behind and touched the tassel on His robe, 21 for
she said to herself, "If I can just touch His robe, I'll be made well!"

22 But Jesus turned and saw her. "Have courage,
daughter," He said. "Your faith has made you well." And
the woman was made well from that moment.

23 When Jesus came to the leader's house, He saw the flute players and
a crowd lamenting loudly. 24 "Leave," He said, "because the girl isn't
dead, but sleeping." And they started laughing at Him. 25 But when the
crowd had been put outside, He went in and took her by the hand, and
the girl got up. 26 And this news spread throughout that whole area.

Healing the Blind

27 As Jesus went on from there, two blind men followed
Him, shouting, "Have mercy on us, Son of David!"

28 When He entered the house, the blind men approached Him,
and Jesus said to them, "Do you believe that I can do this?"

"Yes, Lord," they answered Him.

29 Then He touched their eyes, saying, "Let it be done for you
according to your faith!" 30 And their eyes were opened. Then Jesus
warned them sternly, "Be sure that no one finds out!" 31 But they went
out and spread the news about Him throughout that whole area.

Driving Out a Demon

32 Just as they were going out, a demon-possessed man who was
unable to speak was brought to Him. 33 When the demon had
been driven out, the man spoke. And the crowds were amazed,
saying, "Nothing like this has ever been seen in Israel!"

34 But the Pharisees said, "He drives out
demons by the ruler of the demons!"

The Lord of the Harvest

35 Then Jesus went to all the towns and villages, teaching in their
synagogues, preaching the good news of the kingdom, and healing
every disease and every sickness. 36 When He saw the crowds, He
felt compassion for them, because they were weary and worn out,
like sheep without a shepherd. 37 Then He said to His disciples, "The
harvest is abundant, but the workers are few. 38 Therefore, pray
to the Lord of the harvest to send out workers into His harvest."

<u>Mediate.</u>

Jesus knows how much faith I have.

Jesus knows how much faith I could have.

Jesus still forgives sins.

Jesus helps people.

Jesus can help me.

Jesus sees and knows me.

What could I do for Jesus?

Not everyone will like me.

What do I need to get rid of?

What does Jesus need to help me with?

Am I glad for my relationship with Jesus?

Can God use me now?

Jesus helps me now.

You can laugh at Jesus now, but one day you will not?

What do I need to do for Jesus now?

What do I need to learn from Jesus now?

Is Jesus my teacher?

Am I working for Jesus or Satan?

9

COMMISSIONING THE TWELVE

1 Summoning His 12 disciples, He gave them authority over
unclean spirits, to drive them out and to heal every disease
and sickness. 2 These are the names of the 12 apostles:
First, Simon, who is called Peter,
and Andrew his brother;
James the son of Zebedee,
and John his brother;

3 Philip and Bartholomew;
Thomas and Matthew the tax collector;
James the son of Alphaeus, and Thaddaeus;

4 Simon the Zealot, and Judas Iscariot,
who also betrayed Him.

5 Jesus sent out these 12 after giving them instructions: "Don't take
the road leading to other nations, and don't enter any Samaritan
town. 6 Instead, go to the lost sheep of the house of Israel. 7 As
you go, announce this: 'The kingdom of heaven has come near.'
8 Heal the sick, raise the dead, cleanse those with skin diseases,
drive out demons. You have received free of charge; give free of
charge. 9 Don't take along gold, silver, or copper for your money-
belts. 10 Don't take a traveling bag for the road, or an extra shirt,
sandals, or a walking stick, for the worker is worthy of his food.

11 "When you enter any town or village, find out who is worthy, and
stay there until you leave. 12 Greet a household when you enter it,
13 and if the household is worthy, let your peace be on it. But if it is
unworthy, let your peace return to you. 14 If anyone will not welcome
you or listen to your words, shake the dust off your feet when you leave
that house or town. 15 I assure you: It will be more tolerable on the day
of judgment for the land of Sodom and Gomorrah than for that town.

Persecutions Predicted

16 "Look, I'm sending you out like sheep among wolves. Therefore be
as shrewd as serpents and as harmless as doves. 17 Because people
will hand you over to sanhedrins and flog you in their synagogues,
beware of them. 18 You will even be brought before governors and
kings because of Me, to bear witness to them and to the nations. 19 But
when they hand you over, don't worry about how or what you should
speak. For you will be given what to say at that hour, 20 because you
are not speaking, but the Spirit of your Father is speaking through you.

21 "Brother will betray brother to death, and a father his child.
Children will even rise up against their parents and have them put
to death. 22 You will be hated by everyone because of My name.
But the one who endures to the end will be delivered. 23 When
they persecute you in one town, escape to another. For I assure
you: You will not have covered the towns of Israel before the Son
of Man comes. 24 A disciple is not above his teacher, or a slave
above his master. 25 It is enough for a disciple to become like his
teacher and a slave like his master. If they called the head of the
house 'Beelzebul,' how much more the members of his household!

Fear God

26 "Therefore, don't be afraid of them, since there is nothing
covered that won't be uncovered and nothing hidden that won't

be made known. 27 What I tell you in the dark, speak in the light. What you hear in a whisper, proclaim on the housetops. 28 Don't fear those who kill the body but are not able to kill the soul; rather, fear Him who is able to destroy both soul and body in hell. 29 Aren't two sparrows sold for a penny? Yet not one of them falls to the ground without your Father's consent. 30 But even the hairs of your head have all been counted. 31 So don't be afraid therefore; you are worth more than many sparrows.

Acknowledging Christ

32 "Therefore, everyone who will acknowledge Me before men, I will also acknowledge him before My Father in heaven. 33 But whoever denies Me before men, I will also deny him before My Father in heaven. 34 Don't assume that I came to bring peace on the earth. I did not come to bring peace, but a sword. 35 For I came to turn
a man against his father,
a daughter against her mother,
a daughter-in-law against her mother-in-law;

36 and a man's enemies will be

the members of his household.

37 The person who loves father or mother more than Me is not worthy of Me; the person who loves son or daughter more than Me is not worthy of Me. 38 And whoever doesn't take up his cross and follow Me is not worthy of Me. 39 Anyone finding his life will lose it, and anyone losing his life because of Me will find it.

A Cup of Cold Water

40 "The one who welcomes you welcomes Me, and the one who welcomes Me welcomes Him who sent Me. 41 Anyone who welcomes a prophet because he is a prophet will receive a prophet's reward. And anyone who welcomes a righteous person because he's righteous will receive a righteous person's reward. 42 And whoever gives just a cup of cold water to one of these little ones because he is a disciple — I assure you: He will never lose his reward!"

Mediation time.

Jesus still empowers.

With Jesus' help I can do amazing things.

Jesus knows my name, and everything about me.

Jesus is coming soon.

Money isn't my greatest need.

How important is the Bible to me?

Not everyone loves the Bible.

I need to be wise.

Jesus can help me through the tough times.

How and who hates us is a true test of how good of a Christian I am.

Do I suffer as a Christian?

My real enemy is Satan.

Do I confess Jesus to others?

I am in a real war for souls.

I have a cross to bear.

How do I treat other Christians?

What do I give to others?

What rewards await me in heaven?

In chapters 11-20, I shall use the New King James Bible

10

John the Baptist Sends Messengers to Jesus

*11 Now it came to pass, when Jesus finished
commanding His twelve disciples, that He departed
from there to teach and to preach in their cities.*

*2 And when John had heard in prison about the works of
Christ, he [a]sent two of his disciples 3 and said to Him,
"Are You the Coming One, or do we look for another?"*

*4 Jesus answered and said to them, "Go and tell John the
things which you hear and see: 5 The blind see and the lame
walk; the lepers are cleansed and the deaf hear; the dead are
raised up and the poor have the gospel preached to them. 6
And blessed is he who is not offended because of Me."*

*7 As they departed, Jesus began to say to the multitudes concerning
John: "What did you go out into the wilderness to see? A reed shaken
by the wind? 8 But what did you go out to see? A man clothed in
soft garments? Indeed, those who wear soft clothing are in kings'
houses. 9 But what did you go out to see? A prophet? Yes, I say to you,
and more than a prophet. 10 For this is he of whom it is written:*

*'Behold, I send My messenger before Your face,
Who will prepare Your way before You.'*

11 "Assuredly, I say to you, among those born of women there has
not risen one greater than John the Baptist; but he who is least in
the kingdom of heaven is greater than he. 12 And from the days of
John the Baptist until now the kingdom of heaven suffers violence,
and the violent take it by force. 13 For all the prophets and the law
prophesied until John. 14 And if you are willing to receive it, he is
Elijah who is to come. 15 He who has ears to hear, let him hear!

16 "But to what shall I liken this generation? It is like children sitting
in the marketplaces and calling to their companions, 17 and saying:

'We played the flute for you,
And you did not dance;
We mourned to you,
And you did not [b]lament.'

18 For John came neither eating nor drinking, and they say, 'He
has a demon.' 19 The Son of Man came eating and drinking, and
they say, 'Look, a glutton and a [c]winebibber, a friend of tax
collectors and sinners!' But wisdom is justified by her [d]children."

Woe to the Impenitent Cities

20 Then He began to rebuke the cities in which most of His mighty
works had been done, because they did not repent: 21 "Woe to you,
Chorazin! Woe to you, Bethsaida! For if the mighty works which
were done in you had been done in Tyre and Sidon, they would have
repented long ago in sackcloth and ashes. 22 But I say to you, it will
be more tolerable for Tyre and Sidon in the day of judgment than
for you. 23 And you, Capernaum, who[e] are exalted to heaven,
will be brought down to Hades; for if the mighty works which were
done in you had been done in Sodom, it would have remained
until this day. 24 But I say to you that it shall be more tolerable
for the land of Sodom in the day of judgment than for you."

Jesus Gives True Rest

25 At that time Jesus answered and said, "I thank You, Father, Lord of heaven and earth, that You have hidden these things from the wise and prudent and have revealed them to babes. 26 Even so, Father, for so it seemed good in Your sight. 27 All things have been delivered to Me by My Father, and no one knows the Son except the Father. Nor does anyone know the Father except the Son, and the one to whom the Son wills to reveal Him. 28 Come to Me, all you who labor and are heavy laden, and I will give you rest. 29 Take My yoke upon you and learn from Me, for I am [f]gentle and lowly in heart, and you will find rest for your souls. 30 For My yoke is easy and My burden is light."

Mediate.

I need to learn the truth.

My actions speak louder than my words.

Who have I helped today?

What I believe about Jesus matters eternally.

Others watch me closely.

Opinions matter, but the one that counts is God's.

Others do watch me closely.

Bad days lie ahead if I ignore the gospel.

I need to humble myself and learn.

I need to take my problems to Jesus.

What could I learn from Jesus?

Do I rest in Jesus?

Real peace comes from knowing and trusting Jesus.

11

Lord of the Sabbath

1 At that time Jesus passed through the grainfields on the Sabbath.
His disciples were hungry and began to pick and eat some heads
of grain. 2 But when the Pharisees saw it, they said to Him, "Look,
Your disciples are doing what is not lawful to do on the Sabbath!"

3 He said to them, "Haven't you read what David did when he and
those who were with him were hungry — 4 how he entered the house
of God, and they ate the sacred bread, which is not lawful for him
or for those with him to eat, but only for the priests? 5 Or haven't
you read in the Law that on Sabbath days the priests in the temple
violate the Sabbath and are innocent? 6 But I tell you that something
greater than the temple is here! 7 If you had known what this means:
I desire mercy and not sacrifice, you would not have condemned
the innocent. 8 For the Son of Man is Lord of the Sabbath."

The Man with the Paralyzed Hand

9 Moving on from there, He entered their synagogue. 10 There
He saw a man who had a paralyzed hand. And in order to accuse
Him they asked Him, "Is it lawful to heal on the Sabbath?"

11 But He said to them, "What man among you, if he had
a sheep that fell into a pit on the Sabbath, wouldn't take
hold of it and lift it out? 12 A man is worth far more than a
sheep, so it is lawful to do what is good on the Sabbath."

*13 Then He told the man, "Stretch out your hand." So he stretched
it out, and it was restored, as good as the other. 14 But the Pharisees
went out and plotted against Him, how they might destroy Him.*

The Servant of the Lord

*15 When Jesus became aware of this, He withdrew from there.
Huge crowds followed Him, and He healed them all. 16 He
warned them not to make Him known, 17 so that what was
spoken through the prophet Isaiah might be fulfilled:*

*18 Here is My Servant whom I have chosen,
My beloved in whom My soul delights;
I will put My Spirit on Him,
and He will proclaim justice to the nations.*

*19 He will not argue or shout,
and no one will hear His voice in the streets.*

*20 He will not break a bruised reed,
and He will not put out a smoldering wick,
until He has led justice to victory.*

21 The nations will put their hope in His name.

A House Divided

*22 Then a demon-possessed man who was blind and unable
to speak was brought to Him. He healed him, so that the
man could both speak and see. 23 And all the crowds were
astounded and said, "Perhaps this is the Son of David!"*

*24 When the Pharisees heard this, they said, "The man drives
out demons only by Beelzebul, the ruler of the demons."*

25 Knowing their thoughts, He told them: "Every kingdom divided
against itself is headed for destruction, and no city or house divided
against itself will stand. 26 If Satan drives out Satan, he is divided
against himself. How then will his kingdom stand? 27 And if I drive
out demons by Beelzebul, who is it your sons drive them out by? For
this reason they will be your judges. 28 If I drive out demons by the
Spirit of God, then the kingdom of God has come to you. 29 How can
someone enter a strong man's house and steal his possessions unless
he first ties up the strong man? Then he can rob his house. 30 Anyone
who is not with Me is against Me, and anyone who does not gather
with Me scatters. 31 Because of this, I tell you, people will be forgiven
every sin and blasphemy, but the blasphemy against the Spirit will
not be forgiven. 32 Whoever speaks a word against the Son of Man,
it will be forgiven him. But whoever speaks against the Holy Spirit,
it will not be forgiven him, either in this age or in the one to come.

A Tree and Its Fruit

33 "Either make the tree good and its fruit good, or make the tree
bad and its fruit bad; for a tree is known by its fruit. 34 Brood
of vipers! How can you speak good things when you are evil?
For the mouth speaks from the overflow of the heart. 35 A good
man produces good things from his storeroom of good, and an
evil man produces evil things from his storeroom of evil. 36 I tell
you that on the day of judgment people will have to account for
every careless word they speak. 37 For by your words you will
be acquitted, and by your words you will be condemned."

The Sign of Jonah

38 Then some of the scribes and Pharisees said to Him,
"Teacher, we want to see a sign from You."

39 But He answered them, "An evil and adulterous generation
demands a sign, but no sign will be given to it except the sign of
the prophet Jonah. 40 For as Jonah was in the belly of the huge fish
three days and three nights, so the Son of Man will be in the heart
of the earth three days and three nights. 41 The men of Nineveh
will stand up at the judgment with this generation and condemn
it, because they repented at Jonah's proclamation; and look —
something greater than Jonah is here! 42 The queen of the south
will rise up at the judgment with this generation and condemn it,
because she came from the ends of the earth to hear the wisdom of
Solomon; and look — something greater than Solomon is here!

An Unclean Spirit's Return

43 "When an unclean spirit comes out of a man, it roams through
waterless places looking for rest but doesn't find any. 44 Then it says,
'I'll go back to my house that I came from.' And returning, it finds
the house vacant, swept, and put in order. 45 Then off it goes and
brings with it seven other spirits more evil than itself, and they enter
and settle down there. As a result, that man's last condition is worse
than the first. That's how it will also be with this evil generation."

True Relationships

46 He was still speaking to the crowds when suddenly His
mother and brothers were standing outside wanting to speak
to Him. 47 Someone told Him, "Look, Your mother and Your
brothers are standing outside, wanting to speak to You."

48 But He replied to the one who told Him, "Who is My
mother and who are My brothers?" 49 And stretching out His
hand toward His disciples, He said, "Here are My mother and
My brothers! 50 For whoever does the will of My Father in
heaven, that person is My brother and sister and mother."

<u>Mediation time.</u>

A big part of our fellowship is eating together.

God's house is important.

What am I doing to help God's house?

Jesus is lord of all.

How do I help others?

How do I make Jesus known?

The Old Testament helps us to understand the New Testament.

I can trust Jesus.

Jesus' power is of God for He is God in the flesh.

Jesus knows my thoughts.

Am I for Jesus or not?

What I say is very important.

Jesus' deeds tell us who He is.

Demons are real.

Family is important, but Jesus is more important.

Am I a part of the family of God?

12

The Parable of the Sower

13 On the same day Jesus went out of the house and sat by the sea. 2
And great multitudes were gathered together to Him, so that He got
into a boat and sat; and the whole multitude stood on the shore.

3 Then He spoke many things to them in parables, saying: "Behold,
a sower went out to sow. 4 And as he sowed, some seed fell by
the wayside; and the birds came and devoured them. 5 Some fell
on stony places, where they did not have much earth; and they
immediately sprang up because they had no depth of earth. 6
But when the sun was up they were scorched, and because they
had no root they withered away. 7 And some fell among thorns,
and the thorns sprang up and choked them. 8 But others fell
on good ground and yielded a crop: some a hundredfold, some
sixty, some thirty. 9 He who has ears to hear, let him hear!"

The Purpose of Parables

10 And the disciples came and said to Him, "Why
do You speak to them in parables?"

11 He answered and said to them, "Because it has been given
to you to know the [a]mysteries of the kingdom of heaven, but
to them it has not been given. 12 For whoever has, to him more
will be given, and he will have abundance; but whoever does
not have, even what he has will be taken away from him. 13
Therefore I speak to them in parables, because seeing they do not

see, and hearing they do not hear, nor do they understand. 14
And in them the prophecy of Isaiah is fulfilled, which says:

'Hearing you will hear and shall not understand,
And seeing you will see and not perceive;

15 For the hearts of this people have grown dull.
Their ears are hard of hearing,
And their eyes they have closed,
Lest they should see with their eyes and hear with their ears,
Lest they should understand with their hearts and turn,
So that I [b]should heal them.'

16 But blessed are your eyes for they see, and your ears for
they hear; 17 for assuredly, I say to you that many prophets
and righteous men desired to see what you see, and did not
see it, and to hear what you hear, and did not hear it.

The Parable of the Sower Explained

18 "Therefore hear the parable of the sower: 19 When anyone hears
the word of the kingdom, and does not understand it, then the wicked
one comes and snatches away what was sown in his heart. This is
he who received seed by the wayside. 20 But he who received the
seed on stony places, this is he who hears the word and immediately
receives it with joy; 21 yet he has no root in himself, but endures
only for a while. For when tribulation or persecution arises because
of the word, immediately he stumbles. 22 Now he who received
seed among the thorns is he who hears the word, and the cares of
this world and the deceitfulness of riches choke the word, and he
becomes unfruitful. 23 But he who received seed on the good ground
is he who hears the word and understands it, who indeed bears
fruit and produces: some a hundredfold, some sixty, some thirty."

The Parable of the Wheat and the Tares

24 Another parable He put forth to them, saying: "The kingdom of heaven is like a man who sowed good seed in his field; 25 but while men slept, his enemy came and sowed tares among the wheat and went his way. 26 But when the grain had sprouted and produced a crop, then the tares also appeared. 27 So the servants of the owner came and said to him, 'Sir, did you not sow good seed in your field? How then does it have tares?' 28 He said to them, 'An enemy has done this.' The servants said to him, 'Do you want us then to go and gather them up?' 29 But he said, 'No, lest while you gather up the tares you also uproot the wheat with them. 30 Let both grow together until the harvest, and at the time of harvest I will say to the reapers, "First gather together the tares and bind them in bundles to burn them, but gather the wheat into my barn." '"

The Parable of the Mustard Seed

31 Another parable He put forth to them, saying: "The kingdom of heaven is like a mustard seed, which a man took and sowed in his field, 32 which indeed is the least of all the seeds; but when it is grown it is greater than the herbs and becomes a tree, so that the birds of the air come and nest in its branches."

The Parable of the Leaven

33 Another parable He spoke to them: "The kingdom of heaven is like leaven, which a woman took and hid in three [c]measures of meal till it was all leavened."

Prophecy and the Parables

34 All these things Jesus spoke to the multitude in parables; and without a parable He did not speak to them, 35 that it might be fulfilled which was spoken by the prophet, saying:

"I will open My mouth in parables;
I will utter things kept secret from the foundation of the world."

The Parable of the Tares Explained

36 Then Jesus sent the multitude away and went into
the house. And His disciples came to Him, saying,
"Explain to us the parable of the tares of the field."

37 He answered and said to them: "He who sows the good seed is the
Son of Man. 38 The field is the world, the good seeds are the sons
of the kingdom, but the tares are the sons of the wicked one. 39 The
enemy who sowed them is the devil, the harvest is the end of the age,
and the reapers are the angels. 40 Therefore as the tares are gathered
and burned in the fire, so it will be at the end of this age. 41 The
Son of Man will send out His angels, and they will gather out of His
kingdom all things that offend, and those who practice lawlessness, 42
and will cast them into the furnace of fire. There will be wailing and
gnashing of teeth. 43 Then the righteous will shine forth as the sun in
the kingdom of their Father. He who has ears to hear, let him hear!

The Parable of the Hidden Treasure

44 "Again, the kingdom of heaven is like treasure hidden
in a field, which a man found and hid; and for joy over it
he goes and sells all that he has and buys that field.

The Parable of the Pearl of Great Price

45 "Again, the kingdom of heaven is like a merchant seeking
beautiful pearls, 46 who, when he had found one pearl of
great price, went and sold all that he had and bought it.

The Parable of the Dragnet

*47 "Again, the kingdom of heaven is like a dragnet that was
cast into the sea and gathered some of every kind, 48 which,
when it was full, they drew to shore; and they sat down and
gathered the good into vessels, but threw the bad away. 49 So it
will be at the end of the age. The angels will come forth, separate
the wicked from among the just, 50 and cast them into the
furnace of fire. There will be wailing and gnashing of teeth."*

*51 [d]Jesus said to them, "Have you understood all these things?"
They said to Him, "Yes, [e]Lord."*

*52 Then He said to them, "Therefore every [f]scribe instructed
[g]concerning the kingdom of heaven is like a householder
who brings out of his treasure things new and old."*

Jesus Rejected at Nazareth

*53 Now it came to pass, when Jesus had finished these parables,
that He departed from there. 54 When He had come to His own
country, He taught them in their synagogue, so that they were
astonished and said, "Where did this Man get this wisdom and
these mighty works? 55 Is this not the carpenter's son? Is not His
mother called Mary? And His brothers James, [h]Joses, Simon, and
Judas? 56 And His sisters, are they not all with us? Where then did
this Man get all these things?" 57 So they were offended at Him.*

*But Jesus said to them, "A prophet is not without honor except
in his own country and in his own house." 58 Now He did not
do many mighty works there because of their unbelief.*

Mediate on these.

People need to hear what Jesus said and did.

Jesus often told short stories that had a strong point.

Jesus was a masterful storyteller using familiar objects.

Jesus made people think.

Jesus challenged people to listen.

Am I closed minded?

Some parables Jesus explained, some not.

God can take a little and make it much.

Jesus knows the future.

Jesus can use me now.

What do I treasure?

I need to learn from Jesus' teachings.

Do I know who Jesus is?

What could Jesus do?

13

John the Baptist Beheaded

14 At that time Herod the tetrarch heard the report about Jesus
2 and said to his servants, "This is John the Baptist; he is risen
from the dead, and therefore these powers are at work in him."
3 For Herod had laid hold of John and bound him, and put him
in prison for the sake of Herodias, his brother Philip's wife. 4
Because John had said to him, "It is not lawful for you to have
her." 5 And although he wanted to put him to death, he feared
the multitude, because they counted him as a prophet.

6 But when Herod's birthday was celebrated, the daughter of
Herodias danced before them and pleased Herod. 7 Therefore he
promised with an oath to give her whatever she might ask.

8 So she, having been prompted by her mother, said,
"Give me John the Baptist's head here on a platter."

9 And the king was sorry; nevertheless, because of the oaths
and because of those who sat with him, he commanded it to be
given to her. 10 So he sent and had John beheaded in prison.
11 And his head was brought on a platter and given to the girl,
and she brought it to her mother. 12 Then his disciples came and
took away the body and buried it, and went and told Jesus.

Feeding the Five Thousand

13 When Jesus heard it, He departed from there by boat to a deserted place by Himself. But when the multitudes heard it, they followed Him on foot from the cities. 14 And when Jesus went out He saw a great multitude; and He was moved with compassion for them, and healed their sick. 15 When it was evening, His disciples came to Him, saying, "This is a deserted place, and the hour is already late. Send the multitudes away, that they may go into the villages and buy themselves food."

16 But Jesus said to them, "They do not need to go away. You give them something to eat."

17 And they said to Him, "We have here only five loaves and two fish."

18 He said, "Bring them here to Me." 19 Then He commanded the multitudes to sit down on the grass. And He took the five loaves and the two fish, and looking up to heaven, He blessed and broke and gave the loaves to the disciples; and the disciples gave to the multitudes. 20 So they all ate and were filled, and they took up twelve baskets full of the fragments that remained. 21 Now those who had eaten were about five thousand men, besides women and children.

Jesus Walks on the Sea

22 Immediately Jesus [a]made His disciples get into the boat and go before Him to the other side, while He sent the multitudes away. 23 And when He had sent the multitudes away, He went up on the mountain by Himself to pray. Now when evening came, He was alone there. 24 But the boat was now [b]in the middle of the sea, tossed by the waves, for the wind was contrary.

25 Now in the fourth watch of the night Jesus went to them, walking
on the sea. 26 And when the disciples saw Him walking on the sea,
they were troubled, saying, "It is a ghost!" And they cried out for fear.

27 But immediately Jesus spoke to them, saying, [c]"Be
of good cheer! [d]It is I; do not be afraid."

28 And Peter answered Him and said, "Lord, if it is
You, command me to come to You on the water."

29 So He said, "Come." And when Peter had come down out
of the boat, he walked on the water to go to Jesus. 30 But when
he saw [e]that the wind was boisterous, he was afraid; and
beginning to sink he cried out, saying, "Lord, save me!"

31 And immediately Jesus stretched out His hand and caught
him, and said to him, "O you of little faith, why did you doubt?"
32 And when they got into the boat, the wind ceased.

33 Then those who were in the boat [f]came and worshiped
Him, saying, "Truly You are the Son of God."

Many Touch Him and Are Made Well

34 When they had crossed over, they came [g]to the land of
Gennesaret. 35 And when the men of that place recognized Him, they
sent out into all that surrounding region, brought to Him all who
were sick, 36 and begged Him that they might only touch the hem of
His garment. And as many as touched it were made perfectly well.

<u>Mediation time.</u>

What have I heard about Jesus?

Can I take criticism?

Sin demands a big loss for me.

Jesus cares about happens to us.

Jesus dealt with grief by helping others.

Jesus can make much from a little.

Jesus has much for me to do.

If Jesus needed to pray perhaps, I need too.

Jesus is lord even over nature.

Jesus can help us to do the impossible.

I need to worship Jesus.

Jesus still heals.

I need to stay in touch with Jesus.

Jesus can help me to be my best.

14

Defilement Comes from Within

15 Then the scribes and Pharisees who were from Jerusalem came
to Jesus, saying, 2 "Why do Your disciples transgress the tradition of
the elders? For they do not wash their hands when they eat bread."

3 He answered and said to them, "Why do you also transgress
the commandment of God because of your tradition? 4 For God
commanded, saying, 'Honor your father and your mother'; and,
'He who curses father or mother, let him be put to death.' 5 But
you say, 'Whoever says to his father or mother, "Whatever profit
you might have received from me is a gift to God"— 6 then he
need not honor his father [a]or mother.' Thus you have made
the [b]commandment of God of no effect by your tradition. 7
Hypocrites! Well did Isaiah prophesy about you, saying:

8 'These people [c]draw near to Me with their mouth,
And honor Me with their lips,
But their heart is far from Me.

9 And in vain they worship Me,
Teaching as doctrines the commandments of men.'"

10 When He had called the multitude to Himself, He said to them,
"Hear and understand: 11 Not what goes into the mouth defiles
a man; but what comes out of the mouth, this defiles a man."

12 Then His disciples came and said to Him, "Do You know that
the Pharisees were offended when they heard this saying?"

13 But He answered and said, "Every plant which My
heavenly Father has not planted will be uprooted. 14 Let
them alone. They are blind leaders of the blind. And if
the blind leads the blind, both will fall into a ditch."

15 Then Peter answered and said to Him, "Explain this parable to us."

16 So Jesus said, "Are you also still without understanding? 17 Do
you not yet understand that whatever enters the mouth goes into the
stomach and is eliminated? 18 But those things which proceed out of
the mouth come from the heart, and they defile a man. 19 For out of
the heart proceed evil thoughts, murders, adulteries, fornications,
thefts, false witness, blasphemies. 20 These are the things which defile
a man, but to eat with unwashed hands does not defile a man."

A Gentile Shows Her Faith

21 Then Jesus went out from there and departed to the region of
Tyre and Sidon. 22 And behold, a woman of Canaan came from
that region and cried out to Him, saying, "Have mercy on me, O
Lord, Son of David! My daughter is severely demon-possessed."

23 But He answered her not a word.
And His disciples came and urged Him, saying,
"Send her away, for she cries out after us."

24 But He answered and said, "I was not sent except
to the lost sheep of the house of Israel."

25 Then she came and worshiped Him, saying, "Lord, help me!"

26 But He answered and said, "It is not good to take the children's bread and throw it to the little dogs."

27 And she said, "Yes, Lord, yet even the little dogs eat the crumbs which fall from their masters' table."

28 Then Jesus answered and said to her, "O woman, great is your faith! Let it be to you as you desire." And her daughter was healed from that very hour.

Jesus Heals Great Multitudes

*29 Jesus departed from there, skirted the Sea of Galilee, and went
up on the mountain and sat down there. 30 Then great multitudes
came to Him, having with them the lame, blind, mute, [d]maimed,
and many others; and they laid them down at Jesus' feet, and He
healed them. 31 So the multitude marveled when they saw the
mute speaking, the [e]maimed made whole, the lame walking,
and the blind seeing; and they glorified the God of Israel.*

Feeding the Four Thousand

32 Now Jesus called His disciples to Himself and said, "I have compassion on the multitude, because they have now continued with Me three days and have nothing to eat. And I do not want to send them away hungry, lest they faint on the way."

33 Then His disciples said to Him, "Where could we get enough bread in the wilderness to fill such a great multitude?"

34 Jesus said to them, "How many loaves do you have?" And they said, "Seven, and a few little fish."

*35 So He commanded the multitude to sit down on the ground. 36 And
He took the seven loaves and the fish and gave thanks, broke them and*

gave them to His disciples; and the disciples gave to the multitude. 37
So they all ate and were filled, and they took up seven large baskets
full of the fragments that were left. 38 Now those who ate were four
thousand men, besides women and children. 39 And He sent away the
multitude, got into the boat, and came to the region of [f]Magdala.

Mediate.

Just how important are man's rules?

Do I look for loopholes?

Do I honor my parents?

Do I only have a mouth religion?

Do my words and actions agree?

Why do I worship the lord?

How do I worship the lord?

What do I think about?

Do I have time to help others?

When is the last time I had a good talk with Jesus?

Do I ask the lord for his help?

If I do as Jesus says, will I be better off?

Can I move on, or do I dwell too long on some things?

15

THE PHARISEES AND SADDUCEES SEEK A SIGN

16 Then the Pharisees and Sadducees came, and testing Him asked
that He would show them a sign from heaven. 2 He answered and
said to them, "When it is evening you say, 'It will be fair weather,
for the sky is red'; 3 and in the morning, 'It will be foul weather
today, for the sky is red and threatening.' [a]Hypocrites! You
know how to discern the face of the sky, but you cannot discern
the signs of the times. 4 A wicked and adulterous generation
seeks after a sign, and no sign shall be given to it except the sign
of [b]the prophet Jonah." And He left them and departed.

The Leaven of the Pharisees and Sadducees

5 Now when His disciples had come to the other side, they had
forgotten to take bread. 6 Then Jesus said to them, "Take heed and
beware of the [c]leaven of the Pharisees and the Sadducees."

7 And they reasoned among themselves, saying,
"It is because we have taken no bread."

8 But Jesus, being aware of it, said to them, "O you of little
faith, why do you reason among yourselves because you
[d]have brought no bread? 9 Do you not yet understand,
or remember the five loaves of the five thousand and how
many baskets you took up? 10 Nor the seven loaves of the

four thousand and how many large baskets you took up?
11 How is it you do not understand that I did not speak to
you concerning bread?—but to beware of the [e]leaven of
the Pharisees and Sadducees." 12 Then they understood
that He did not tell them to beware of the leaven of bread,
but of the [f]doctrine of the Pharisees and Sadducees.

Peter Confesses Jesus as the Christ

13 When Jesus came into the region of Caesarea Philippi, He asked
His disciples, saying, "Who do men say that I, the Son of Man, am?"

14 So they said, "Some say John the Baptist, some Elijah,
and others Jeremiah or one of the prophets."

15 He said to them, "But who do you say that I am?"

16 Simon Peter answered and said, "You are
the Christ, the Son of the living God."

17 Jesus answered and said to him, "Blessed are you, Simon
Bar-Jonah, for flesh and blood has not revealed this to you,
but My Father who is in heaven. 18 And I also say to you
that you are Peter, and on this rock I will build My church,
and the gates of Hades shall not [g]prevail against it. 19
And I will give you the keys of the kingdom of heaven, and
whatever you bind on earth [h]will be bound in heaven,
and whatever you loose on earth will be loosed in heaven."

20 Then He commanded His disciples that they should
tell no one that He was Jesus the Christ.

Jesus Predicts His Death and Resurrection

*21 From that time Jesus began to show to His
disciples that He must go to Jerusalem, and suffer
many things from the elders and chief priests and
scribes, and be killed, and be raised the third day.*

*22 Then Peter took Him aside and began to rebuke Him, saying,
[i]"Far be it from You, Lord; this shall not happen to You!"*

*23 But He turned and said to Peter, "Get behind Me,
Satan! You are [j]an offense to Me, for you are not
mindful of the things of God, but the things of men."*

Take Up the Cross and Follow Him

*24 Then Jesus said to His disciples, "If anyone desires to come
after Me, let him deny himself, and take up his cross, and follow
Me. 25 For whoever desires to save his life will lose it, but whoever
loses his life for My sake will find it. 26 For what profit is it to
a man if he gains the whole world, and loses his own soul? Or
what will a man give in exchange for his soul? 27 For the Son of
Man will come in the glory of His Father with His angels, and
then He will reward each according to his works. 28 Assuredly,
I say to you, there are some standing here who shall not taste
death till they see the Son of Man coming in His kingdom."*

<u>Time to mediate.</u>

What do I demand from God?

What am I missing?

Just how much faith do I have?

What might help my faith to grow?

Does the Holy Spirit guide me?

Who is Jesus to me?

Am I greatly influenced by what people think.

What am I building my life on?

Bad things happen to bad people.

Bad things happen to good people.

Can I deny myself?

How is my soul?

What will my reward look like?

Am I ready if Jesus comes now?

16

Jesus Transfigured on the Mount

17 Now after six days Jesus took Peter, James, and John his brother,
led them up *on a high mountain by themselves; 2 and He was*
transfigured before them. His face shone like the sun, and His clothes
became as white as the light. 3 And behold, Moses and Elijah appeared
to them, talking with Him. 4 Then Peter answered and said to Jesus,
"Lord, it is good for us to be here; if You wish, [a]let us make here
three tabernacles: one for You, one for Moses, and one for Elijah."

5 While he was still speaking, behold, a bright cloud overshadowed
them; and suddenly a voice came out of the cloud, saying, "This is My
beloved Son, in whom I am well pleased. Hear Him!" 6 And when the
disciples heard it, they fell on their faces and were greatly afraid. 7 But
Jesus came and touched them and said, "Arise, and do not be afraid."
8 When they had lifted up their eyes, they saw no one but Jesus only.

9 Now as they came down from the mountain, Jesus
commanded them, saying, "Tell the vision to no one
until the Son of Man is risen from the dead."

10 And His disciples asked Him, saying, "Why then
do the scribes say that Elijah must come first?"

11 Jesus answered and said to them, "Indeed, Elijah is coming
[b]first and will restore all things. 12 But I say to you that

Elijah has come already, and they did not know him but did to him whatever they wished. Likewise the Son of Man is also about to suffer at their hands." 13 Then the disciples understood that He spoke to them of John the Baptist.

A Boy Is Healed

14 And when they had come to the multitude, a man came to Him, kneeling down to Him and saying, 15 "Lord, have mercy on my son, for he is [c]an epileptic and suffers severely; for he often falls into the fire and often into the water. 16 So I brought him to Your disciples, but they could not cure him."

17 Then Jesus answered and said, "O [d]faithless and perverse generation, how long shall I be with you? How long shall I bear with you? Bring him here to Me." 18 And Jesus rebuked the demon, and it came out of him; and the child was cured from that very hour.

19 Then the disciples came to Jesus privately and said, "Why could we not cast it out?"

20 So Jesus said to them, "Because of your [e]unbelief; for assuredly, I say to you, if you have faith as a mustard seed, you will say to this mountain, 'Move from here to there,' and it will move; and nothing will be impossible for you. 21 [f]However, this kind does not go out except by prayer and fasting."

Jesus Again Predicts His Death and Resurrection

22 Now while they were [g]staying in Galilee, Jesus said to them, "The Son of Man is about to be betrayed into the hands of men, 23 and they will kill Him, and the third day He will be raised up." And they were exceedingly sorrowful.

Peter and His Master Pay Their Taxes

24 When they had come to [h]Capernaum, those who received the [i]temple tax came to Peter and said, "Does your Teacher not pay the temple tax?"

25 He said, "Yes."

And when he had come into the house, Jesus anticipated him, saying, "What do you think, Simon? From whom do the kings of the earth take customs or taxes, from their sons or from strangers?"

26 Peter said to Him, "From strangers."

Jesus said to him, "Then the sons are free. 27 Nevertheless, lest we offend them, go to the sea, cast in a hook, and take the fish that comes up first. And when you have opened its mouth, you will find a [j]piece of money; take that and give it to them for Me and you."

<u>Meditation time</u>

Where might Jesus send me?

There is more than life on earth.

One day I will know more than I know now.

Jesus wants me to not fear.

Somethings I will not know till I arrive in heaven.

I need to keep my eyes on Jesus.

Listening to Jesus will help me to learn helpful things.

I need to take my problems to Jesus.

Prayer is powerful.

Not many fast.

We hear what we want to hear.

Jesus valued children.

Good things happen when I listen to Jesus.

17

WHO IS THE GREATEST?

18 At that time the disciples came to Jesus, saying, "Who then is greatest in the kingdom of heaven?"

2 Then Jesus called a little child to Him, set him in the midst of
them, 3 and said, "Assuredly, I say to you, unless you are converted
and become as little children, you will by no means enter the
kingdom of heaven. 4 Therefore whoever humbles himself as this
little child is the greatest in the kingdom of heaven. 5 Whoever
receives one little child like this in My name receives Me.

Jesus Warns of Offenses

6 "But whoever causes one of these little ones who believe in
Me to sin, it would be better for him if a millstone were hung
around his neck, and he were drowned in the depth of the sea.
7 Woe to the world because of [a]offenses! For offenses must
come, but woe to that man by whom the offense comes!

8 "If your hand or foot causes you to sin, cut it off and cast it
from you. It is better for you to enter into life lame or maimed,
rather than having two hands or two feet, to be cast into the
everlasting fire. 9 And if your eye causes you to sin, pluck it out
and cast it from you. It is better for you to enter into life with one
eye, rather than having two eyes, to be cast into [b]hell fire.

The Parable of the Lost Sheep

10 "Take heed that you do not despise one of these little
ones, for I say to you that in heaven their angels always
see the face of My Father who is in heaven. 11 For[c] the
Son of Man has come to save that which was lost.

12 "What do you think? If a man has a hundred sheep, and
one of them goes astray, does he not leave the ninety-nine
and go to the mountains to seek the one that is straying? 13
And if he should find it, assuredly, I say to you, he rejoices
more over that sheep than over the ninety-nine that did
not go astray. 14 Even so it is not the will of your Father
who is in heaven that one of these little ones should perish.

Dealing with a Sinning Brother

15 "Moreover if your brother sins against you, go and tell him
his fault between you and him alone. If he hears you, you have
gained your brother. 16 But if he will not hear, take with you
one or two more, that 'by the mouth of two or three witnesses
every word may be established.' 17 And if he refuses to hear
them, tell it to the church. But if he refuses even to hear the
church, let him be to you like a heathen and a tax collector.

18 "Assuredly, I say to you, whatever you bind
on earth will be bound in heaven, and whatever
you loose on earth will be loosed in heaven.

19 "Again[d] I say to you that if two of you agree on earth
concerning anything that they ask, it will be done for them by
My Father in heaven. 20 For where two or three are gathered
together in My name, I am there in the midst of them."

The Parable of the Unforgiving Servant

21 Then Peter came to Him and said, "Lord, how often shall my
brother sin against me, and I forgive him? Up to seven times?"

22 Jesus said to him, "I do not say to you, up to seven times, but up
to seventy times seven. 23 Therefore the kingdom of heaven is like a
certain king who wanted to settle accounts with his servants. 24 And
when he had begun to settle accounts, one was brought to him who
owed him ten thousand talents. 25 But as he was not able to pay,
his master commanded that he be sold, with his wife and children
and all that he had, and that payment be made. 26 The servant
therefore fell down before him, saying, 'Master, have patience with
me, and I will pay you all.' 27 Then the master of that servant was
moved with compassion, released him, and forgave him the debt.

28 "But that servant went out and found one of his fellow servants
who owed him a hundred denarii; and he laid hands on him and
took him by the throat, saying, 'Pay me what you owe!' 29 So his
fellow servant fell down [e]at his feet and begged him, saying, 'Have
patience with me, and I will pay you [f]all.' 30 And he would not,
but went and threw him into prison till he should pay the debt. 31
So when his fellow servants saw what had been done, they were very
grieved, and came and told their master all that had been done. 32
Then his master, after he had called him, said to him, 'You wicked
servant! I forgave you all that debt because you begged me. 33 Should
you not also have had compassion on your fellow servant, just as
I had pity on you?' 34 And his master was angry, and delivered
him to the torturers until he should pay all that was due to him.

35 "So My heavenly Father also will do to you if each of you,
from his heart, does not forgive his brother [g]his trespasses."

Mediate on these thoughts.

How does one become great?

Not everyone is going to heaven.

It is dangerous not to come to Jesus.

We all need to greatly value children.

Angels are real.

Jesus came to save people.

I am of great value to God.

God intends that we be at peace with each other.

There is a right way to settle issues.

God gave the church great powers.

Agreeing with others can help cause miracles.

If we gather in Jesus' name, He is there.

Can I forgive?

Do I have any unconfessed sins?

What do I owe the lord?

Can I be nice, and forgive others?

We all answer to the lord.

God forgives us as we forgive others.

18

Marriage and Divorce

19 Now it came to pass, when Jesus had finished these sayings, that He departed from Galilee and came to the region of Judea beyond the Jordan. 2 And great multitudes followed Him, and He healed them there.

3 The Pharisees also came to Him, testing Him, and saying to Him, "Is it lawful for a man to divorce his wife for just any reason?"

4 And He answered and said to them, "Have you not read that He who [a]made them at the beginning 'made them male and female,' 5 and said, 'For this reason a man shall leave his father and mother and be joined to his wife, and the two shall become one flesh'? 6 So then, they are no longer two but one flesh. Therefore what God has joined together, let not man separate."

7 They said to Him, "Why then did Moses command to give a certificate of divorce, and to put her away?"

8 He said to them, "Moses, because of the hardness of your hearts, permitted you to divorce your wives, but from the beginning it was not so. 9 And I say to you, whoever divorces his wife, except for [b]sexual immorality, and marries another, commits adultery; and whoever marries her who is divorced commits adultery."

10 His disciples said to Him, "If such is the case of the man with his wife, it is better not to marry."

Jesus Teaches on Celibacy

11 But He said to them, "All cannot accept this saying, but only those to whom it has been given: 12 For there are [c]eunuchs who were born thus from their mother's womb, and there are eunuchs who were made eunuchs by men, and there are eunuchs who have made themselves eunuchs for the kingdom of heaven's sake. He who is able to accept it, let him accept it."

Jesus Blesses Little Children

13 Then little children were brought to Him that He might put His hands on them and pray, but the disciples rebuked them. 14 But Jesus said, "Let the little children come to Me, and do not forbid them; for of such is the kingdom of heaven." 15 And He laid His hands on them and departed from there.

Jesus Counsels the Rich Young Ruler

16 Now behold, one came and said to Him, "Good[d] Teacher, what good thing shall I do that I may have eternal life?"

17 So He said to him, [e]"Why do you call Me good? [f] No one is good but One, that is, God. But if you want to enter into life, keep the commandments."

18 He said to Him, "Which ones?"

Jesus said, "'You shall not murder,' 'You shall not commit adultery,' 'You shall not steal,' 'You shall not bear false witness,' 19 'Honor your father and your mother,' and, 'You shall love your neighbor as yourself.'"

20 The young man said to Him, "All these things I have kept [g]from my youth. What do I still lack?"

21 Jesus said to him, "If you want to be perfect, go, sell what you have and give to the poor, and you will have treasure in heaven; and come, follow Me."

22 But when the young man heard that saying, he went away sorrowful, for he had great possessions.

With God All Things Are Possible

23 Then Jesus said to His disciples, "Assuredly, I say to you that
it is hard for a rich man to enter the kingdom of heaven. 24 And
again I say to you, it is easier for a camel to go through the eye of a needle than for a rich man to enter the kingdom of God."

25 When His disciples heard it, they were greatly astonished, saying, "Who then can be saved?"

26 But Jesus looked at them and said to them, "With men this is impossible, but with God all things are possible."

27 Then Peter answered and said to Him, "See, we have left all and followed You. Therefore what shall we have?"

28 So Jesus said to them, "Assuredly I say to you, that in
the regeneration, when the Son of Man sits on the throne
of His glory, you who have followed Me will also sit on
twelve thrones, judging the twelve tribes of Israel. 29 And
everyone who has left houses or brothers or sisters or father
or mother [h]or wife or children or [i]lands, for My name's
sake, shall receive a hundredfold, and inherit eternal life.
30 But many who are first will be last, and the last first.

Mediate.

Jesus the healer drew crowds.

Jesus talked about important subjects like divorce.

Jesus' desire was to do the will of God.

God loves marriage.

Marriage is to be taken seriously.

Moses tried to please people by allowing divorce.

Fornication and adultery are sins.

Not everyone will marry.

Jesus loved children.

How to have eternal life is a serious subject.

Doing God's will is very important.

Doing good things is wonderful.

What are good things I can do?

Will I allow stuff to keep me from heaven?

God is impressed when we help others.

Why would I help others?

Rich people often love possessions more than God.

With God all things are possible.

God will honor me now and later if I follow Jesus.

Things will be much different in heaven.

19

The Parable of the Workers in the Vineyard

20 "For the kingdom of heaven is like a landowner who went
out early in the morning to hire laborers for his vineyard. 2 Now
when he had agreed with the laborers for a denarius a day, he
sent them into his vineyard. 3 And he went out about the third
hour and saw others standing idle in the marketplace, 4 and said
to them, 'You also go into the vineyard, and whatever is right I
will give you.' So they went. 5 Again he went out about the sixth
and the ninth hour, and did likewise. 6 And about the eleventh
hour he went out and found others standing [a]idle, and said to
them, 'Why have you been standing here idle all day?' 7 They said
to him, 'Because no one hired us.' He said to them, 'You also go
into the vineyard, [b]and whatever is right you will receive.'

8 "So when evening had come, the owner of the vineyard said to his
steward, 'Call the laborers and give them their wages, beginning
with the last to the first.' 9 And when those came who were hired
about the eleventh hour, they each received a denarius. 10 But
when the first came, they supposed that they would receive more;
and they likewise received each a denarius. 11 And when they had
received it, they [c]complained against the landowner, 12 saying,
'These last men have worked only one hour, and you made them
equal to us who have borne the burden and the heat of the day.' 13
But he answered one of them and said, 'Friend, I am doing you no
wrong. Did you not agree with me for a denarius? 14 Take what is

yours and go your way. I wish to give to this last man the same as to you. 15 Is it not lawful for me to do what I wish with my own things? Or is your eye evil because I am good?' 16 So the last will be first, and the first last. For[d] many are called, but few chosen."

Jesus a Third Time Predicts His Death and Resurrection

17 Now Jesus, going up to Jerusalem, took the twelve disciples aside on the road and said to them, 18 "Behold, we are going up to Jerusalem, and the Son of Man will be betrayed to the chief priests and to the scribes; and they will condemn Him to death, 19 and deliver Him to the Gentiles to mock and to scourge and to crucify. And the third day He will rise again."

Greatness Is Serving

20 Then the mother of Zebedee's sons came to Him with her sons, kneeling down and asking something from Him.

21 And He said to her, "What do you wish?"

She said to Him, "Grant that these two sons of mine may sit, one on Your right hand and the other on the left, in Your kingdom."

22 But Jesus answered and said, "You do not know what you ask. Are you able to drink the cup that I am about to drink, [e] and be baptized with the baptism that I am baptized with?"

They said to Him, "We are able."

23 So He said to them, "You will indeed drink My cup, [f] and be baptized with the baptism that I am baptized with; but to sit on My right hand and on My left is not Mine to give, but it is for those for whom it is prepared by My Father."

*24 And when the ten heard it, they were greatly displeased with the
two brothers. 25 But Jesus called them to Himself and said, "You
know that the rulers of the Gentiles lord it over them, and those
who are great exercise authority over them. 26 Yet it shall not be
so among you; but whoever desires to become great among you, let
him be your servant. 27 And whoever desires to be first among you,
let him be your slave— 28 just as the Son of Man did not come to
be served, but to serve, and to give His life a ransom for many."*

Two Blind Men Receive Their Sight

*29 Now as they went out of Jericho, a great multitude
followed Him. 30 And behold, two blind men sitting by the
road, when they heard that Jesus was passing by, cried out,
saying, "Have mercy on us, O Lord, Son of David!"*

*31 Then the multitude warned them that they should
be quiet; but they cried out all the more, saying,
"Have mercy on us, O Lord, Son of David!"*

*32 So Jesus stood still and called them, and said,
"What do you want Me to do for you?"*

*33 They said to Him, "Lord, that our eyes may be opened."
34 So Jesus had compassion and touched their eyes. And
immediately their eyes received sight, and they followed Him.*

Mediate deeply.

God has entrusted us with very much.

Anyone can work for God, even me.

As time passes, more join in the work.

Soon payday comes.

Few work for the lord.

Jesus knows what lies ahead.

God gives out rewards as He sees fit.

God calls for me to serve Him.

Jesus set me an example as He served others.

Jesus is merciful.

Starting in Matthew 21-28 I shall use the NIV.

JOE PACE

20

Jesus Comes to Jerusalem as King

*21:1 As they approached Jerusalem and came to Bethphage
on the Mount of Olives, Jesus sent two disciples, 2 saying to
them, "Go to the village ahead of you, and at once you will
find a donkey tied there, with her colt by her. Untie them and
bring them to me. 3 If anyone says anything to you, say that
the Lord needs them, and he will send them right away."*

4 This took place to fulfill what was spoken through the prophet:

*5 "Say to Daughter Zion,
'See, your king comes to you,
gentle and riding on a donkey,
and on a colt, the foal of a donkey.'"[a]*

*6 The disciples went and did as Jesus had instructed them. 7 They
brought the donkey and the colt and placed their cloaks on them for
Jesus to sit on. 8 A very large crowd spread their cloaks on the road,
while others cut branches from the trees and spread them on the road.
9 The crowds that went ahead of him and those that followed shouted,*

*"Hosanna[b] to the Son of David!"
"Blessed is he who comes in the name of the Lord!"[c]
"Hosanna[d] in the highest heaven!"*

10 When Jesus entered Jerusalem, the whole city
was stirred and asked, "Who is this?"

11 The crowds answered, "This is Jesus, the
prophet from Nazareth in Galilee."

Jesus at the Temple

12 Jesus entered the temple courts and drove out all who
were buying and selling there. He overturned the tables of the
money changers and the benches of those selling doves. 13 "It
is written," he said to them, "'My house will be called a house
of prayer,'[e] but you are making it 'a den of robbers.'[f]"

14 The blind and the lame came to him at the temple, and he healed
them. 15 But when the chief priests and the teachers of the law saw
the wonderful things he did and the children shouting in the temple
courts, "Hosanna to the Son of David," they were indignant.

16 "Do you hear what these children are saying?" they asked him.
"Yes," replied Jesus, "have you never read,
"'From the lips of children and infants
you, Lord, have called forth your praise'[g]?"

17 And he left them and went out of the city to
Bethany, where he spent the night.

Jesus Curses a Fig Tree

18 Early in the morning, as Jesus was on his way back to the city,
he was hungry. 19 Seeing a fig tree by the road, he went up to it
but found nothing on it except leaves. Then he said to it, "May
you never bear fruit again!" Immediately the tree withered.

20 When the disciples saw this, they were amazed. "How did the fig tree wither so quickly?" they asked.

21 Jesus replied, "Truly I tell you, if you have faith and do not doubt, not only can you do what was done to the fig tree, but also you can say to this mountain, 'Go, throw yourself into the sea,' and it will be done.
22 If you believe, you will receive whatever you ask for in prayer."

The Authority of Jesus Questioned

23 Jesus entered the temple courts, and, while he was teaching, the chief priests and the elders of the people came to him. "By what authority are you doing these things?" they asked. "And who gave you this authority?"

24 Jesus replied, "I will also ask you one question. If you answer me, I will tell you by what authority I am doing
these things. 25 John's baptism—where did it come
from? Was it from heaven, or of human origin?"

They discussed it among themselves and said, "If we say, 'From heaven,' he will ask, 'Then why didn't you believe
him?' 26 But if we say, 'Of human origin'—we are afraid of
the people, for they all hold that John was a prophet."

27 So they answered Jesus, "We don't know."

Then he said, "Neither will I tell you by what authority I am doing these things.

The Parable of the Two Sons

28 "What do you think? There was a man who had two sons. He went to the first and said, 'Son, go and work today in the vineyard.'

29 "'I will not,' he answered, but later he changed his mind and went.

30 "Then the father went to the other son and said the same
thing. He answered, 'I will, sir,' but he did not go.

31 "Which of the two did what his father wanted?"

"The first," they answered.

Jesus said to them, "Truly I tell you, the tax collectors and the
prostitutes are entering the kingdom of God ahead of you. 32 For
John came to you to show you the way of righteousness, and you
did not believe him, but the tax collectors and the prostitutes did.
And even after you saw this, you did not repent and believe him.

The Parable of the Tenants

33 "Listen to another parable: There was a landowner who
planted a vineyard. He put a wall around it, dug a winepress in
it and built a watchtower. Then he rented the vineyard to some
farmers and moved to another place. 34 When the harvest time
approached, he sent his servants to the tenants to collect his fruit.

35 "The tenants seized his servants; they beat one, killed another, and
stoned a third. 36 Then he sent other servants to them, more than
the first time, and the tenants treated them the same way. 37 Last
of all, he sent his son to them. 'They will respect my son,' he said.

38 "But when the tenants saw the son, they said to each other, 'This
is the heir. Come, let's kill him and take his inheritance.' 39 So they
took him and threw him out of the vineyard and killed him.

40 "Therefore, when the owner of the vineyard
comes, what will he do to those tenants?"

41 "He will bring those wretches to a wretched end," they replied, "and he will rent the vineyard to other tenants, who will give him his share of the crop at harvest time."

42 Jesus said to them, "Have you never read in the Scriptures:
"'The stone the builders rejected
has become the cornerstone;
the Lord has done this,
and it is marvelous in our eyes'[h]?

43 "Therefore I tell you that the kingdom of God will be
taken away from you and given to a people who will produce
its fruit. 44 Anyone who falls on this stone will be broken
to pieces; anyone on whom it falls will be crushed."[i]

45 When the chief priests and the Pharisees heard Jesus'
parables, they knew he was talking about them. 46 They
looked for a way to arrest him, but they were afraid of the
crowd because the people held that he was a prophet.

<u>Relax and mediate.</u>

Jesus was a detailed planner.

Jesus gave orders that I need to obey.

Jesus was greatly loved.

God's house is to be a house of prayer.

Jesus still heals.

Jesus had close friends.

Jesus expects results from me.

Jesus loved to teach, what do I love to do?

Jesus often answered a question with a question.

Do I have a good attitude?

Do I gladly work for Jesus?

Jesus was more than a prophet.

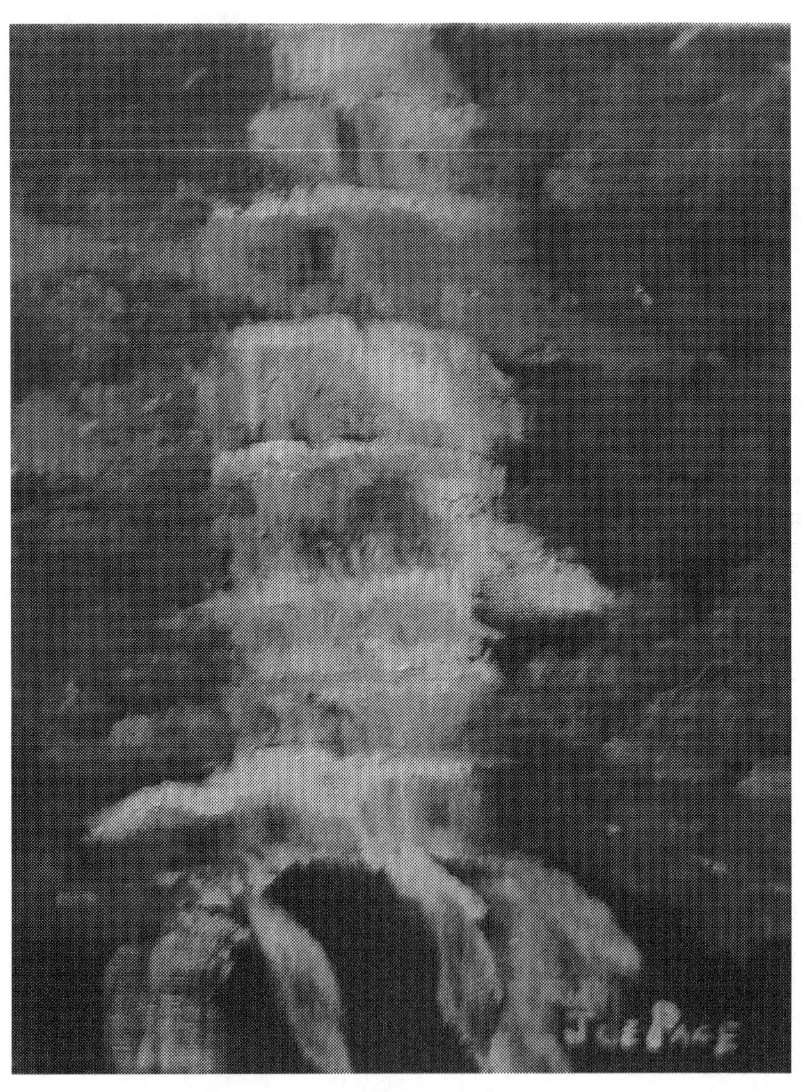

21

The Parable of the Wedding Banquet

22 Jesus spoke to them again in parables, saying: 2 "The kingdom
of heaven is like *a king who prepared a wedding banquet for
his son. 3 He sent his servants to those who had been invited to
the banquet to tell them to come, but they refused to come.*

*4 "Then he sent some more servants and said, 'Tell those
who have been invited that I have prepared my dinner:
My oxen and fattened cattle have been butchered, and
everything is ready. Come to the wedding banquet.'*

*5 "But they paid no attention and went off—one to his field,
another to his business. 6 The rest seized his servants, mistreated
them and killed them. 7 The king was enraged. He sent his
army and destroyed those murderers and burned their city.*

*8 "Then he said to his servants, 'The wedding banquet is ready, but
those I invited did not deserve to come. 9 So go to the street corners
and invite to the banquet anyone you find.' 10 So the servants went
out into the streets and gathered all the people they could find, the
bad as well as the good, and the wedding hall was filled with guests.*

*11 "But when the king came in to see the guests, he noticed a man there
who was not wearing wedding clothes. 12 He asked, 'How did you get
in here without wedding clothes, friend?' The man was speechless.*

13 "Then the king told the attendants, 'Tie him hand and foot, and throw him outside, into the darkness, where there will be weeping and gnashing of teeth.'

14 "For many are invited, but few are chosen."

Paying the Imperial Tax to Caesar

15 Then the Pharisees went out and laid plans to trap him in his words. 16 They sent their disciples to him along with the Herodians. "Teacher," they said, "we know that you are a man of integrity and that you teach the way of God in accordance with the truth. You aren't swayed by others, because you pay no attention to who they are. 17 Tell us then, what is your opinion? Is it right to pay the imperial tax[a] to Caesar or not?"

18 But Jesus, knowing their evil intent, said, "You hypocrites, why are you trying to trap me? 19 Show me the coin used for paying the tax." They brought him a denarius, 20 and he asked them, "Whose image is this? And whose inscription?"

21 "Caesar's," they replied.

Then he said to them, "So give back to Caesar what is Caesar's, and to God what is God's."

22 When they heard this, they were amazed. So they left him and went away.

Marriage at the Resurrection

23 That same day the Sadducees, who say there is no resurrection, came to him with a question. 24 "Teacher," they said, "Moses told us that if a man dies without having children, his brother must marry

*the widow and raise up offspring for him. 25 Now there were seven
brothers among us. The first one married and died, and since he had
no children, he left his wife to his brother. 26 The same thing happened
to the second and third brother, right on down to the seventh. 27
Finally, the woman died. 28 Now then, at the resurrection, whose
wife will she be of the seven, since all of them were married to her?"*

*29 Jesus replied, "You are in error because you do not know
the Scriptures or the power of God. 30 At the resurrection
people will neither marry nor be given in marriage; they will
be like the angels in heaven. 31 But about the resurrection
of the dead—have you not read what God said to you, 32 'I
am the God of Abraham, the God of Isaac, and the God of
Jacob'[b]? He is not the God of the dead but of the living."*

33 When the crowds heard this, they were astonished at his teaching.

The Greatest Commandment

*34 Hearing that Jesus had silenced the Sadducees, the
Pharisees got together. 35 One of them, an expert in
the law, tested him with this question: 36 "Teacher,
which is the greatest commandment in the Law?"*

*37 Jesus replied: "'Love the Lord your God with all your heart
and with all your soul and with all your mind.'[c] 38 This
is the first and greatest commandment. 39 And the second
is like it: 'Love your neighbor as yourself.'[d] 40 All the Law
and the Prophets hang on these two commandments."*

Whose Son Is the Messiah?

*41 While the Pharisees were gathered together, Jesus asked them,
42 "What do you think about the Messiah? Whose son is he?"*

"The son of David," they replied.

43 He said to them, "How is it then that David, speaking by the Spirit, calls him 'Lord'? For he says,

44 "'The Lord said to my Lord:
"Sit at my right hand
until I put your enemies
under your feet."'[e]

45 If then David calls him 'Lord,' how can he be his son?"
46 No one could say a word in reply, and from that day on no one dared to ask him any more questions.

Time to mediate.

Jesus still speaks, I need to listen.

Where might the lord send me?

Not everyone desires to be blessed.

Am I too busy?

Where do I need to go now?

Am I looking for opportunities to witness for Jesus?

Do I have a temper problem?

When was the last time I made a fool of myself?

Do I influence people to do right?

I help the government with my taxes, do I
help my church with my tithes?

When I chose to make Jesus my savior,
I became part of the chosen.

Somethings we need to allow God to handle things.

I enjoy thinking about heaven.

Does it show that I love God?

Jesus was great at answering questions.

Who is Jesus to me?

Who am I to Jesus?

22

A Warning Against Hypocrisy

23 Then Jesus said to the crowds and to his disciples: 2
"The teachers of the law and the Pharisees sit in Moses'
seat. 3 So you must be careful to do everything they tell
you. But do not do what they do, for they do not practice
what they preach. 4 They tie up heavy, cumbersome
loads and put them on other people's shoulders, but they
themselves are not willing to lift a finger to move them.

5 "Everything they do is done for people to see: They
make their phylacteries[a] wide and the tassels on
their garments long; 6 they love the place of honor
at banquets and the most important seats in the
synagogues; 7 they love to be greeted with respect in
the marketplaces and to be called 'Rabbi' by others.

8 "But you are not to be called 'Rabbi,' for you have
one Teacher, and you are all brothers. 9 And do not
call anyone on earth 'father,' for you have one Father,
and he is in heaven. 10 Nor are you to be called
instructors, for you have one Instructor, the Messiah.
11 The greatest among you will be your servant. 12
For those who exalt themselves will be humbled, and
those who humble themselves will be exalted.

Seven Woes on the Teachers of the Law and the Pharisees

13 "Woe to you, teachers of the law and Pharisees, you hypocrites! You
shut the door of the kingdom of heaven in people's faces. You yourselves
do not enter, nor will you let those enter who are trying to. [14] [b]

15 "Woe to you, teachers of the law and Pharisees, you hypocrites! You
travel over land and sea to win a single convert, and when you have
succeeded, you make them twice as much a child of hell as you are.

16 "Woe to you, blind guides! You say, 'If anyone swears by the
temple, it means nothing; but anyone who swears by the gold of the
temple is bound by that oath.' 17 You blind fools! Which is greater:
the gold, or the temple that makes the gold sacred? 18 You also say,
'If anyone swears by the altar, it means nothing; but anyone who
swears by the gift on the altar is bound by that oath.' 19 You blind
men! Which is greater: the gift, or the altar that makes the gift sacred?
20 Therefore, anyone who swears by the altar swears by it and by
everything on it. 21 And anyone who swears by the temple swears
by it and by the one who dwells in it. 22 And anyone who swears
by heaven swears by God's throne and by the one who sits on it.

23 "Woe to you, teachers of the law and Pharisees, you
hypocrites! You give a tenth of your spices—mint, dill and
cumin. But you have neglected the more important matters
of the law—justice, mercy and faithfulness. You should have
practiced the latter, without neglecting the former. 24 You
blind guides! You strain out a gnat but swallow a camel.

25 "Woe to you, teachers of the law and Pharisees, you hypocrites!
You clean the outside of the cup and dish, but inside they are full
of greed and self-indulgence. 26 Blind Pharisee! First clean the
inside of the cup and dish, and then the outside also will be clean.

27 "Woe to you, teachers of the law and Pharisees, you
hypocrites! You are like whitewashed tombs, which look
beautiful on the outside but on the inside are full of the
bones of the dead and everything unclean. 28 In the same
way, on the outside you appear to people as righteous but
on the inside you are full of hypocrisy and wickedness.

29 "Woe to you, teachers of the law and Pharisees, you hypocrites!
You build tombs for the prophets and decorate the graves of the
righteous. 30 And you say, 'If we had lived in the days of our
ancestors, we would not have taken part with them in shedding
the blood of the prophets.' 31 So you testify against yourselves that
you are the descendants of those who murdered the prophets. 32
Go ahead, then, and complete what your ancestors started!

33 "You snakes! You brood of vipers! How will you
escape being condemned to hell? 34 Therefore I am
sending you prophets and sages and teachers. Some of
them you will kill and crucify; others you will flog in
your synagogues and pursue from town to town. 35
And so upon you will come all the righteous blood that
has been shed on earth, from the blood of righteous
Abel to the blood of Zechariah son of Berekiah, whom
you murdered between the temple and the altar. 36
Truly I tell you, all this will come on this generation.

37 "Jerusalem, Jerusalem, you who kill the prophets and stone
those sent to you, how often I have longed to gather your
children together, as a hen gathers her chicks under her wings,
and you were not willing. 38 Look, your house is left to you
desolate. 39 For I tell you, you will not see me again until you
say, 'Blessed is he who comes in the name of the Lord.'[c]"

Mediate.

Jesus spoke to many people.

Do I read my Bible as I should?

Do I live and talk the Bible?

What do my actions show me to be?

Do I try to act like something I am not?

Who is my father-God or Satan?

What has Jesus told me to do?

I realize to be great is to serve others.

The best way to help others is to help them know Jesus as their savior.

Do I see what is best?

Do I value the house of God?

God can clean me up.

By not helping someone are we helping to kill them?

Who have I hurt?

How have I hurt others?

Am I a blessing or a curse to others?

JOE PAGE

23

The Destruction of the Temple and Signs of the End Times

24 Jesus left the temple and was walking away when his disciples
came up to him to call his attention to its buildings. 2 "Do you
see all these things?" he asked. "Truly I tell you, not one stone
here will be left on another; every one will be thrown down."

3 As Jesus was sitting on the Mount of Olives, the disciples came
to him privately. "Tell us," they said, "when will this happen, and
what will be the sign of your coming and of the end of the age?"

4 Jesus answered: "Watch out that no one deceives you. 5 For
many will come in my name, claiming, 'I am the Messiah,' and
will deceive many. 6 You will hear of wars and rumors of wars,
but see to it that you are not alarmed. Such things must happen,
but the end is still to come. 7 Nation will rise against nation, and
kingdom against kingdom. There will be famines and earthquakes
in various places. 8 All these are the beginning of birth pains.

9 "Then you will be handed over to be persecuted and put to death,
and you will be hated by all nations because of me. 10 At that time
many will turn away from the faith and will betray and hate each
other, 11 and many false prophets will appear and deceive many
people. 12 Because of the increase of wickedness, the love of most will
grow cold, 13 but the one who stands firm to the end will be saved.

14 And this gospel of the kingdom will be preached in the whole world as a testimony to all nations, and then the end will come.

*15 "So when you see standing in the holy place 'the abomination that
causes desolation,'[a] spoken of through the prophet Daniel—let the
reader understand— 16 then let those who are in Judea flee to the
mountains. 17 Let no one on the housetop go down to take anything
out of the house. 18 Let no one in the field go back to get their cloak. 19
How dreadful it will be in those days for pregnant women and nursing
mothers! 20 Pray that your flight will not take place in winter or on
the Sabbath. 21 For then there will be great distress, unequaled from
the beginning of the world until now—and never to be equaled again.*

*22 "If those days had not been cut short, no one would survive,
but for the sake of the elect those days will be shortened. 23 At that
time if anyone says to you, 'Look, here is the Messiah!' or, 'There
he is!' do not believe it. 24 For false messiahs and false prophets
will appear and perform great signs and wonders to deceive, if
possible, even the elect. 25 See, I have told you ahead of time.*

*26 "So if anyone tells you, 'There he is, out in the wilderness,'
do not go out; or, 'Here he is, in the inner rooms,' do not believe
it. 27 For as lightning that comes from the east is visible
even in the west, so will be the coming of the Son of Man. 28
Wherever there is a carcass, there the vultures will gather.*

29 "Immediately after the distress of those days
"'the sun will be darkened,
and the moon will not give its light;
the stars will fall from the sky,
and the heavenly bodies will be shaken.'[b]

*30 "Then will appear the sign of the Son of Man in heaven. And then
all the peoples of the earth[c] will mourn when they see the Son of Man*

coming on the clouds of heaven, with power and great glory.[d] 31 And
he will send his angels with a loud trumpet call, and they will gather
his elect from the four winds, from one end of the heavens to the other.

32 "Now learn this lesson from the fig tree: As soon as its twigs get
tender and its leaves come out, you know that summer is near. 33
Even so, when you see all these things, you know that it[e] is near,
right at the door. 34 Truly I tell you, this generation will certainly
not pass away until all these things have happened. 35 Heaven
and earth will pass away, but my words will never pass away.

The Day and Hour Unknown

36 "But about that day or hour no one knows, not even the angels
in heaven, nor the Son,[f] but only the Father. 37 As it was in the
days of Noah, so it will be at the coming of the Son of Man. 38
For in the days before the flood, people were eating and drinking,
marrying and giving in marriage, up to the day Noah entered
the ark; 39 and they knew nothing about what would happen
until the flood came and took them all away. That is how it will
be at the coming of the Son of Man. 40 Two men will be in the
field; one will be taken and the other left. 41 Two women will be
grinding with a hand mill; one will be taken and the other left.

42 "Therefore keep watch, because you do not know on what day
your Lord will come. 43 But understand this: If the owner of the
house had known at what time of night the thief was coming,
he would have kept watch and would not have let his house be
broken into. 44 So you also must be ready, because the Son of
Man will come at an hour when you do not expect him.

45 "Who then is the faithful and wise servant, whom the
master has put in charge of the servants in his household to
give them their food at the proper time? 46 It will be good

for that servant whose master finds him doing so when he returns. 47 Truly I tell you, he will put him in charge of all his possessions. 48 But suppose that servant is wicked and says to himself, 'My master is staying away a long time,' 49 and he then begins to beat his fellow servants and to eat and drink with drunkards. 50 The master of that servant will come on a day when he does not expect him and at an hour he is not aware of. 51 He will cut him to pieces and assign him a place with the hypocrites, where there will be weeping and gnashing of teeth.

Meditation time.

What impresses me?

Do I inspire others?

How do I impress others?

What lasts?

Many desire to be famous.

Jesus is coming soon.

Bad things are happening.

How hated am I?

When was the last time I was made fun of?

There are so many false preachers and teachers today.

Am I helping God's house to be what it should be?

How could I improve my prayer life?

It is now like it was in the days of Noah.

I am ready for Jesus to come again.

What will we do in heaven?

Hell is real and many will go there.

24

The Parable of the Ten Virgins

25 "At that time the kingdom of heaven will be like ten virgins who
took their lamps and went out to meet the bridegroom. 2 Five of
them were foolish and five were wise. 3 The foolish ones took their
lamps but did not take any oil with them. 4 The wise ones, however,
took oil in jars along with their lamps. 5 The bridegroom was a
long time in coming, and they all became drowsy and fell asleep.

6 "At midnight the cry rang out: 'Here's the
bridegroom! Come out to meet him!'

7 "Then all the virgins woke up and trimmed their
lamps. 8 The foolish ones said to the wise, 'Give us
some of your oil; our lamps are going out.'

9 "'No,' they replied, 'there may not be enough for both us and you.
Instead, go to those who sell oil and buy some for yourselves.'

10 "But while they were on their way to buy the oil, the
bridegroom arrived. The virgins who were ready went in with
him to the wedding banquet. And the door was shut.

11 "Later the others also came. 'Lord, Lord,'
they said, 'open the door for us!'

12 "But he replied, 'Truly I tell you, I don't know you.'

13 "Therefore keep watch, because you do not know the day or the hour.

The Parable of the Bags of Gold

14 "Again, it will be like a man going on a journey, who called his servants and entrusted his wealth to them. 15 To one he gave five bags of gold, to another two bags, and to another one bag,[a] each according to his ability. Then he went on his journey. 16 The man who had received five bags of gold went at once and put his money to work and gained five bags more. 17 So also, the one with two bags of gold gained two more. 18 But the man who had received one bag went off, dug a hole in the ground and hid his master's money.

19 "After a long time the master of those servants returned and settled accounts with them. 20 The man who had received five bags of gold brought the other five. 'Master,' he said, 'you entrusted me with five bags of gold. See, I have gained five more.'

21 "His master replied, 'Well done, good and faithful servant! You have been faithful with a few things; I will put you in charge of many things. Come and share your master's happiness!'

22 "The man with two bags of gold also came. 'Master,' he said, 'you entrusted me with two bags of gold; see, I have gained two more.'

23 "His master replied, 'Well done, good and faithful servant! You have been faithful with a few things; I will put you in charge of many things. Come and share your master's happiness!'

24 "Then the man who had received one bag of gold came. 'Master,' he said, 'I knew that you are a hard man, harvesting where you have not sown and gathering where you have not

scattered seed. 25 So I was afraid and went out and hid your
gold in the ground. See, here is what belongs to you.'

26 "His master replied, 'You wicked, lazy servant! So you
knew that I harvest where I have not sown and gather where
I have not scattered seed? 27 Well then, you should have
put my money on deposit with the bankers, so that when I
returned I would have received it back with interest.

28 "'So take the bag of gold from him and give it to the one who has
ten bags. 29 For whoever has will be given more, and they will have
an abundance. Whoever does not have, even what they have will be
taken from them. 30 And throw that worthless servant outside, into
the darkness, where there will be weeping and gnashing of teeth.'

The Sheep and the Goats

31 "When the Son of Man comes in his glory, and all the angels
with him, he will sit on his glorious throne. 32 All the nations
will be gathered before him, and he will separate the people one
from another as a shepherd separates the sheep from the goats.
33 He will put the sheep on his right and the goats on his left.

34 "Then the King will say to those on his right, 'Come, you who
are blessed by my Father; take your inheritance, the kingdom
prepared for you since the creation of the world. 35 For I was
hungry and you gave me something to eat, I was thirsty and you
gave me something to drink, I was a stranger and you invited me
in, 36 I needed clothes and you clothed me, I was sick and you
looked after me, I was in prison and you came to visit me.'

37 "Then the righteous will answer him, 'Lord, when did
we see you hungry and feed you, or thirsty and give you
something to drink? 38 When did we see you a stranger and

invite you in, or needing clothes and clothe you? 39 When did we see you sick or in prison and go to visit you?'

40 "The King will reply, 'Truly I tell you, whatever you did for one of the least of these brothers and sisters of mine, you did for me.'

41 "Then he will say to those on his left, 'Depart from me, you who are cursed, into the eternal fire prepared for the devil and his angels. 42 For I was hungry and you gave me nothing to eat, I was thirsty and you gave me nothing to drink, 43 I was a stranger and you did not invite me in, I needed clothes and you did not clothe me, I was sick and in prison and you did not look after me.'

44 "They also will answer, 'Lord, when did we see you hungry or thirsty or a stranger or needing clothes or sick or in prison, and did not help you?'

45 "He will reply, 'Truly I tell you, whatever you did not do for one of the least of these, you did not do for me.'

46 "Then they will go away to eternal punishment, but the righteous to eternal life."

<u>Learn from these mediations.</u>

Jesus' second coming will be unexpected.

Everyone has talents, even me.

Most will not be ready when Jesus comes again.

When Jesus comes again it will be late to change minds.

We all answer to the lord.

Even nations answer to the lord.

Do I reach out to help others?

Do I visit others?

Our eternity is being shaped now.

25

THE PLOT AGAINST JESUS

26 When Jesus had finished saying all these things, he said to his disciples, 2 "As you know, the Passover is two days away— and the Son of Man will be handed over to be crucified."

3 Then the chief priests and the elders of the people assembled in the palace of the high priest, whose name was Caiaphas, 4 and they schemed to arrest Jesus secretly and kill him. 5 "But not during the festival," they said, "or there may be a riot among the people."

Jesus Anointed at Bethany

6 While Jesus was in Bethany in the home of Simon the Leper, 7 a woman came to him with an alabaster jar of very expensive perfume, which she poured on his head as he was reclining at the table.

8 When the disciples saw this, they were indignant. "Why this waste?" they asked. 9 "This perfume could have been sold at a high price and the money given to the poor."

10 Aware of this, Jesus said to them, "Why are you bothering this woman? She has done a beautiful thing to me. 11 The poor you will always have with you,[a] but you will not always have me. 12 When she poured this perfume on my body, she did it to prepare me for burial. 13 Truly I tell you, wherever this gospel is preached throughout the world, what she has done will also be told, in memory of her."

Judas Agrees to Betray Jesus

14 Then one of the Twelve—the one called Judas Iscariot—went to the
chief priests 15 and asked, "What are you willing to give me if I deliver
him over to you?" So they counted out for him thirty pieces of silver.
16 From then on Judas watched for an opportunity to hand him over.

The Last Supper

17 On the first day of the Festival of Unleavened Bread, the
disciples came to Jesus and asked, "Where do you want us
to make preparations for you to eat the Passover?"

18 He replied, "Go into the city to a certain man and tell him, 'The
Teacher says: My appointed time is near. I am going to celebrate
the Passover with my disciples at your house.'" 19 So the disciples
did as Jesus had directed them and prepared the Passover.

20 When evening came, Jesus was reclining at the table
with the Twelve. 21 And while they were eating, he
said, "Truly I tell you, one of you will betray me."

22 They were very sad and began to say to him one after
the other, "Surely you don't mean me, Lord?"

23 Jesus replied, "The one who has dipped his hand into the bowl
with me will betray me. 24 The Son of Man will go just as it is
written about him. But woe to that man who betrays the Son
of Man! It would be better for him if he had not been born."

25 Then Judas, the one who would betray him,
said, "Surely you don't mean me, Rabbi?"

Jesus answered, "You have said so."

26 While they were eating, Jesus took bread, and when
he had given thanks, he broke it and gave it to his
disciples, saying, "Take and eat; this is my body."

27 Then he took a cup, and when he had given thanks, he gave it to
them, saying, "Drink from it, all of you. 28 This is my blood of the[b]
covenant, which is poured out for many for the forgiveness of sins.
29 I tell you, I will not drink from this fruit of the vine from now on
until that day when I drink it new with you in my Father's kingdom."

30 When they had sung a hymn, they went out to the Mount of Olives.

Jesus Predicts Peter's Denial

31 Then Jesus told them, "This very night you will all
fall away on account of me, for it is written:

"'I will strike the shepherd,

and the sheep of the flock will be scattered.'[c]

32 But after I have risen, I will go ahead of you into Galilee."

33 Peter replied, "Even if all fall away on account of you, I never will."

34 "Truly I tell you," Jesus answered, "this very night, before
the rooster crows, you will disown me three times."

35 But Peter declared, "Even if I have to die with you, I will
never disown you." And all the other disciples said the same.

Gethsemane

36 Then Jesus went with his disciples to a place called
Gethsemane, and he said to them, "Sit here while I go over

there and pray." 37 He took Peter and the two sons of Zebedee
along with him, and he began to be sorrowful and troubled. 38
Then he said to them, "My soul is overwhelmed with sorrow
to the point of death. Stay here and keep watch with me."

39 Going a little farther, he fell with his face to the ground and prayed, "My Father, if it is possible, may this cup be taken from me. Yet not as I will, but as you will."

40 Then he returned to his disciples and found them sleeping.
"Couldn't you men keep watch with me for one hour?" he
asked Peter. 41 "Watch and pray so that you will not fall into
temptation. The spirit is willing, but the flesh is weak."

42 He went away a second time and prayed, "My Father, if it is not possible for this cup to be taken away unless I drink it, may your will be done."

43 When he came back, he again found them sleeping, because
their eyes were heavy. 44 So he left them and went away once
more and prayed the third time, saying the same thing.

45 Then he returned to the disciples and said to them,
"Are you still sleeping and resting? Look, the hour has
come, and the Son of Man is delivered into the hands of
sinners. 46 Rise! Let us go! Here comes my betrayer!"

Jesus Arrested

47 While he was still speaking, Judas, one of the Twelve, arrived. With
him was a large crowd armed with swords and clubs, sent from the
chief priests and the elders of the people. 48 Now the betrayer had
arranged a signal with them: "The one I kiss is the man; arrest him." 49
Going at once to Jesus, Judas said, "Greetings, Rabbi!" and kissed him.

50 Jesus replied, "Do what you came for, friend."[d]

Then the men stepped forward, seized Jesus and arrested him. 51
With that, one of Jesus' companions reached for his sword, drew it
out and struck the servant of the high priest, cutting off his ear.

52 "Put your sword back in its place," Jesus said to him, "for
all who draw the sword will die by the sword. 53 Do you think I
cannot call on my Father, and he will at once put at my disposal
more than twelve legions of angels? 54 But how then would the
Scriptures be fulfilled that say it must happen in this way?"

55 In that hour Jesus said to the crowd, "Am I leading a rebellion,
that you have come out with swords and clubs to capture me? Every
day I sat in the temple courts teaching, and you did not arrest me.
56 But this has all taken place that the writings of the prophets
might be fulfilled." Then all the disciples deserted him and fled.

Jesus Before the Sanhedrin

57 Those who had arrested Jesus took him to Caiaphas the high priest,
where the teachers of the law and the elders had assembled. 58 But
Peter followed him at a distance, right up to the courtyard of the high
priest. He entered and sat down with the guards to see the outcome.

59 The chief priests and the whole Sanhedrin were looking for false
evidence against Jesus so that they could put him to death. 60 But
they did not find any, though many false witnesses came forward.

Finally two came forward 61 and declared, "This fellow said, 'I am
able to destroy the temple of God and rebuild it in three days.'"

62 Then the high priest stood up and said to Jesus, "Are you not going to answer? What is this testimony that these men are bringing against you?" 63 But Jesus remained silent.

The high priest said to him, "I charge you under oath by the living God: Tell us if you are the Messiah, the Son of God."

64 "You have said so," Jesus replied. "But I say to all of you: From now on you will see the Son of Man sitting at the right hand of the Mighty One and coming on the clouds of heaven."[e]

65 Then the high priest tore his clothes and said, "He has spoken blasphemy! Why do we need any more witnesses? Look, now you have heard the blasphemy. 66 What do you think?"

"He is worthy of death," they answered.

67 Then they spit in his face and struck him with their fists. Others slapped him 68 and said, "Prophesy to us, Messiah. Who hit you?"

Peter Disowns Jesus

69 Now Peter was sitting out in the courtyard, and a servant girl came to him. "You also were with Jesus of Galilee," she said.

70 But he denied it before them all. "I don't know what you're talking about," he said.

71 Then he went out to the gateway, where another servant girl saw him and said to the people there, "This fellow was with Jesus of Nazareth."

72 He denied it again, with an oath: "I don't know the man!"

73 After a little while, those standing there went up to Peter and said, "Surely you are one of them; your accent gives you away."

74 Then he began to call down curses, and he swore to them, "I don't know the man!"

Immediately a rooster crowed.
75 Then Peter remembered the word Jesus had spoken: "Before the rooster crows, you will disown me three times." And he went outside and wept bitterly.

<u>Mediate.</u>

Jesus knows the future.

Some hate Jesus.

What have I done lately to show I love Jesus.

Do I sacrifice for Jesus?

Would I sell out Jesus?

Jesus was the ultimate sacrifice.

Eating together is a treasure.

Jesus knows me and you.

Jesus knew how to answer questions.

The lord's supper is a very special time.

How do I praise the lord?

Prayer is very important.

I need to do what Jesus says.

Satan wins brief battles, but Jesus is the victor.

Friends sometimes aren't friends.

Jesus is in charge.

The Bible is always right.

Buildings are nice, but Jesus is better.

What others think, may not be the best.

Like Peter have I ever denied Jesus.

How emotional is my relationship with Jesus?

26

Judas Hangs Himself

27 Early in the morning, all the chief priests and the elders of the people made their plans how to have Jesus executed. 2 So they bound him, led him away and handed him over to Pilate the governor.

3 When Judas, who had betrayed him, saw that Jesus was condemned, he was seized with remorse and returned the thirty pieces of silver to the chief priests and the elders. 4 "I have sinned," he said, "for I have betrayed innocent blood."

"What is that to us?" they replied. "That's your responsibility."

5 So Judas threw the money into the temple and left. Then he went away and hanged himself.

6 The chief priests picked up the coins and said, "It is against the law to put this into the treasury, since it is blood money." 7 So they decided to use the money to buy the potter's field as a burial place for foreigners. 8 That is why it has been called the Field of Blood to this day. 9 Then what was spoken by Jeremiah the prophet was fulfilled: "They took the thirty pieces of silver, the price set on him by the people of Israel, 10 and they used them to buy the potter's field, as the Lord commanded me."[a]

Jesus Before Pilate

11 Meanwhile Jesus stood before the governor, and the governor asked him, "Are you the king of the Jews?"

"You have said so," Jesus replied.

12 When he was accused by the chief priests and the elders, he gave no answer. 13 Then Pilate asked him, "Don't you hear the testimony they are bringing against you?" 14 But Jesus made no reply, not even to a single charge—to the great amazement of the governor.

15 Now it was the governor's custom at the festival to release a prisoner chosen by the crowd. 16 At that time they had a well-known prisoner whose name was Jesus[b] Barabbas. 17 So when the crowd had gathered, Pilate asked them, "Which one do you want me to release to you: Jesus Barabbas, or Jesus who is called the Messiah?" 18 For he knew it was out of self-interest that they had handed Jesus over to him.

19 While Pilate was sitting on the judge's seat, his wife sent him this message: "Don't have anything to do with that innocent man, for I have suffered a great deal today in a dream because of him."

20 But the chief priests and the elders persuaded the crowd to ask for Barabbas and to have Jesus executed.

21 "Which of the two do you want me to release to you?" asked the governor.

"Barabbas," they answered.

22 "What shall I do, then, with Jesus who is called the Messiah?" Pilate asked.

They all answered, "Crucify him!"

23 "Why? What crime has he committed?" asked Pilate.

But they shouted all the louder, "Crucify him!"

24 When Pilate saw that he was getting nowhere, but that instead an uproar was starting, he took water and washed his hands in front of the crowd. "I am innocent of this man's blood," he said. "It is your responsibility!"

25 All the people answered, "His blood is on us and on our children!"

26 Then he released Barabbas to them. But he had Jesus flogged, and handed him over to be crucified.

The Soldiers Mock Jesus

27 Then the governor's soldiers took Jesus into the Praetorium
and gathered the whole company of soldiers around him. 28 They
stripped him and put a scarlet robe on him, 29 and then twisted
together a crown of thorns and set it on his head. They put a staff
in his right hand. Then they knelt in front of him and mocked
him. "Hail, king of the Jews!" they said. 30 They spit on him, and
took the staff and struck him on the head again and again. 31
After they had mocked him, they took off the robe and put his
own clothes on him. Then they led him away to crucify him.

The Crucifixion of Jesus

32 As they were going out, they met a man from Cyrene, named
Simon, and they forced him to carry the cross. 33 They came to a
place called Golgotha (which means "the place of the skull"). 34
There they offered Jesus wine to drink, mixed with gall; but after
tasting it, he refused to drink it. 35 When they had crucified him,

they divided up his clothes by casting lots. 36 And sitting down,
they kept watch over him there. 37 Above his head they placed the
written charge against him: this is jesus, the king of the jews.

38 Two rebels were crucified with him, one on his right
and one on his left. 39 Those who passed by hurled insults
at him, shaking their heads 40 and saying, "You who are
going to destroy the temple and build it in three days,
save yourself! Come down from the cross, if you are the
Son of God!" 41 In the same way the chief priests, the
teachers of the law and the elders mocked him. 42 "He
saved others," they said, "but he can't save himself! He's
the king of Israel! Let him come down now from the
cross, and we will believe in him. 43 He trusts in God.
Let God rescue him now if he wants him, for he said, 'I
am the Son of God.'" 44 In the same way the rebels who
were crucified with him also heaped insults on him.

The Death of Jesus

45 From noon until three in the afternoon darkness came over
all the land. 46 About three in the afternoon Jesus cried out
in a loud voice, "Eli, Eli,[c] lema sabachthani?" (which means
"My God, my God, why have you forsaken me?").[d]

47 When some of those standing there heard
this, they said, "He's calling Elijah."

48 Immediately one of them ran and got a sponge. He filled it with
wine vinegar, put it on a staff, and offered it to Jesus to drink. 49 The
rest said, "Now leave him alone. Let's see if Elijah comes to save him."

50 And when Jesus had cried out again in a
loud voice, he gave up his spirit.

51 At that moment the curtain of the temple was torn in two from top to bottom. The earth shook, the rocks split 52 and the tombs broke open. The bodies of many holy people who had died were raised to life. 53 They came out of the tombs after Jesus' resurrection and[e] went into the holy city and appeared to many people.

54 When the centurion and those with him who were guarding Jesus saw the earthquake and all that had happened, they were terrified, and exclaimed, "Surely he was the Son of God!"

55 Many women were there, watching from a distance. They had followed Jesus from Galilee to care for his needs. 56 Among them were Mary Magdalene, Mary the mother of James and Joseph,[f] and the mother of Zebedee's sons.

The Burial of Jesus

57 As evening approached, there came a rich man from Arimathea, named Joseph, who had himself become a disciple of Jesus. 58 Going to Pilate, he asked for Jesus' body, and Pilate ordered that it be given to him. 59 Joseph took the body, wrapped it in a clean linen cloth, 60 and placed it in his own new tomb that he had cut out of the rock. He rolled a big stone in front of the entrance to the tomb and went away. 61 Mary Magdalene and the other Mary were sitting there opposite the tomb.

The Guard at the Tomb

62 The next day, the one after Preparation Day, the chief priests and the Pharisees went to Pilate. 63 "Sir," they said, "we remember that while he was still alive that deceiver said, 'After three days I will rise again.' 64 So give the order for the tomb to be made secure until the third day. Otherwise, his disciples may come and steal the body and tell the people that he has been raised from the dead. This last deception will be worse than the first."

65 "Take a guard," Pilate answered. "Go, make the tomb as secure as you know how." 66 So they went and made the tomb secure by putting a seal on the stone and posting the guard.

Mediation time

Why would anyone hate me?

Has anyone ever been mean to me?

Have I ever been mean to someone?

Have I sold out for money?

Where will I be buried?

What do others think about me?

It would be wise to listen to our mates.

Wrong choices can be made.

Is someone's blood on my hands?

What am I waiting for?

Religious people can be wrong.

What am I watching for?

God doesn't like to look on sin.

One day all graves will be empty.

Can others count on me when the chips are down?

Who can we count on when the chips are down?

What do our actions tell other people?

27

Jesus Has Risen

28 After the Sabbath, at dawn on the first day of the week, Mary
Magdalene and *the other Mary went to look at the tomb.*

*2 There was a violent earthquake, for an angel of the Lord
came down from heaven and, going to the tomb, rolled back
the stone and sat on it. 3 His appearance was like lightning,
and his clothes were white as snow. 4 The guards were so
afraid of him that they shook and became like dead men.*

*5 The angel said to the women, "Do not be afraid, for I know that you
are looking for Jesus, who was crucified. 6 He is not here; he has risen,
just as he said. Come and see the place where he lay. 7 Then go quickly
and tell his disciples: 'He has risen from the dead and is going ahead
of you into Galilee. There you will see him.' Now I have told you."*

*8 So the women hurried away from the tomb, afraid yet filled
with joy, and ran to tell his disciples. 9 Suddenly Jesus met them.
"Greetings," he said. They came to him, clasped his feet and
worshiped him. 10 Then Jesus said to them, "Do not be afraid. Go
and tell my brothers to go to Galilee; there they will see me."*

The Guards' Report

*11 While the women were on their way, some of the guards went
into the city and reported to the chief priests everything that had
happened. 12 When the chief priests had met with the elders and*

devised a plan, they gave the soldiers a large sum of money, 13
telling them, "You are to say, 'His disciples came during the night
and stole him away while we were asleep.' 14 If this report gets to the
governor, we will satisfy him and keep you out of trouble." 15 So the
soldiers took the money and did as they were instructed. And this
story has been widely circulated among the Jews to this very day.

The Great Commission

16 Then the eleven disciples went to Galilee, to the mountain where
Jesus had told them to go. 17 When they saw him, they worshiped
him; but some doubted. 18 Then Jesus came to them and said,
"All authority in heaven and on earth has been given to me. 19
Therefore go and make disciples of all nations, baptizing them in
the name of the Father and of the Son and of the Holy Spirit, 20
and teaching them to obey everything I have commanded you.
And surely I am with you always, to the very end of the age."

Mediation.

Close friends are precious and few.

Nature answers to God.

Angels are real. One third are bad, the rest belong to God.

Jesus came out of the grave.

Jesus desires that we worship Him.

Jesus wants me to not be afraid.

Lies are told, many believed.

We need to go where Jesus wants us to go.

Some doubted after seeing the risen Jesus,

Jesus has all power in heaven and earth.

Jesus has things He wants us to do:

1. Go everywhere.
2. Teach people the truth.
3. Baptize new believers.
4. Teach all Jesus commanded.
5. Realize He will always be with us.

Amen-so be it.

Going deeper

In this section you will be challenged to go through Matthew 5

verse by verse slowly allowing the Holy Spirit
to speak to you one verse at a time.

You will have some space in between to jot your notes if needed.

We will be using the HCSB version.

The Sermon on the Mount- Matthew 5

Allow me to do this first verse to give you my example.

1 When He saw the crowds, He went up on the mountain, and after He sat down, His disciples came to Him. Jesus saw people-do we notice people?

Jesus went where he could be heard. Notice He sat down-the custom in those days- the teacher sat down the audience stood up. People wanted to learn from Jesus, what can we teach others?

Your time.

1 When He saw the crowds, He went up on the mountain,
and after He sat down, His disciples came to Him.

2 Then He began to teach them, saying:

The Beatitudes

3 "The poor in spirit are blessed,
for the kingdom of heaven is theirs.

4 Those who mourn are blessed,
for they will be comforted.

5 The gentle are blessed,
for they will inherit the earth.

6 Those who hunger and thirst for righteousness are blessed,
for they will be filled.

7 The merciful are blessed,
for they will be shown mercy.

8 The pure in heart are blessed,
for they will see God.

9 The peacemakers are blessed,
for they will be called sons of God.

*10 Those who are persecuted for righteousness are blessed,
for the kingdom of heaven is theirs.*

*11 "You are blessed when they insult and persecute you and
falsely say every kind of evil against you because of Me.*

*12 Be glad and rejoice, because your reward is great in heaven. For
that is how they persecuted the prophets who were before you.*

Believers Are Salt and Light

*13 "You are the salt of the earth. But if the salt should lose
its taste, how can it be made salty? It's no longer good for
anything but to be thrown out and trampled on by men.*

*14 "You are the light of the world. A city situated on a hill cannot
be hidden. 15 No one lights a lamp and puts it under a basket, but
rather on a lampstand, and it gives light for all who are in the house.
16 In the same way, let your light shine before men, so that they
may see your good works and give glory to your Father in heaven.*

Christ Fulfills the Law

*17 "Don't assume that I came to destroy the Law or the
Prophets. I did not come to destroy but to fulfill.*

*18 For I assure you: Until heaven and earth pass away,
not the smallest letter or one stroke of a letter will pass
from the law until all things are accomplished.*

*19 Therefore, whoever breaks one of the least of these
commands and teaches people to do so will be called least in
the kingdom of heaven. But whoever practices and teaches these
commands will be called great in the kingdom of heaven.*

20 For I tell you, unless your righteousness surpasses that of the scribes and Pharisees, you will never enter the kingdom of heaven.

Murder Begins in the Heart

21 "You have heard that it was said to our ancestors, Do not murder, and whoever murders will be subject to judgment.

22 But I tell you, everyone who is angry with his brother will be subject to judgment. And whoever says to his brother, 'Fool!' will be subject to the Sanhedrin. But whoever says, 'You moron!' will be subject to hellfire.

23 So if you are offering your gift on the altar, and there you remember that your brother has something against you,

24 leave your gift there in front of the altar. First go and be reconciled with your brother, and then come and offer your gift.

25 Reach a settlement quickly with your adversary while you're on the way with him, or your adversary will hand you over to the judge, the judge to the officer, and you will be thrown into prison.

26 I assure you: You will never get out of there until you have paid the last penny!

Adultery in the Heart

27 "You have heard that it was said, Do not commit adultery.
28 But I tell you, everyone who looks at a woman to lust for her has already committed adultery with her in his heart.

29 If your right eye causes you to sin, gouge it out and throw it away. For it is better that you lose one of the parts of your body than for your whole body to be thrown into hell.

30 And if your right hand causes you to sin, cut it off and throw it away. For it is better that you lose one of the parts of your body than for your whole body to go into hell!

Divorce Practices Censured

31 "It was also said, Whoever divorces his wife must give her a written notice of divorce.

32 But I tell you, everyone who divorces his wife, except in a case of sexual immorality, causes her to commit adultery. And whoever marries a divorced woman commits adultery.

Tell the Truth

33 "Again, you have heard that it was said to our ancestors, You must not break your oath, but you must keep your oaths to the Lord.

34 But I tell you, don't take an oath at all: either by heaven, because it is God's throne;

35 or by the earth, because it is His footstool; or by Jerusalem, because it is the city of the great King.

36 Neither should you swear by your head, because you cannot make a single hair white or black.

37 But let your word 'yes' be 'yes,' and your 'no' be 'no.' Anything more than this is from the evil one.

Go the Second Mile

38 "You have heard that it was said, An eye for an eye and a tooth for a tooth.

39 But I tell you, don't resist an evildoer. On the contrary, if anyone slaps you on your right cheek, turn the other to him also.

40 As for the one who wants to sue you and take away your shirt, let him have your coat as well.

41 And if anyone forces you to go one mile, go with him two.

42 Give to the one who asks you, and don't turn away from the one who wants to borrow from you.

Love Your Enemies

43 "You have heard that it was said, Love your neighbor and hate your enemy.

44 But I tell you, love your enemies and pray for those who persecute you,

45 so that you may be sons of your Father in heaven. For He causes His sun to rise on the evil and the good, and sends rain on the righteous and the unrighteous.

46 For if you love those who love you, what reward will you have? Don't even the tax collectors do the same?

47 And if you greet only your brothers, what are you doing out of the ordinary? Don't even the Gentiles do the same?

48 Be perfect, therefore, as your heavenly Father is perfect.

Has God used this to teach you more about Him and yourself?

If so, that was the goal of this book.

My next book which should be out soon will be "Getting closer to God by Studying the Bible Better".

Printed in the United States
by Baker & Taylor Publisher Services